JOURNEY OF
FORGIVENESS

JOURNEY OF FORGIVENESS

BY BARBARA HOWARD

Christian Education Commission
Reorganized Church of Jesus Christ of Latter Day Saints
Herald Publishing House

Printed in the United States of America

Library of Congress Cataloging in Publication Data

Howard, Barbara, 1930-
   The Journey of Forgiveness.

   Bibliography: p.
   1. Forgiveness—Religious   aspects—Christianity.
2. Spiritual life—Mormon authors. I. Title.
BV4647.F55H69   1986   241'.4   86-20770
ISBN 0-8309-0463-8

94   93   92   91   4   5   6   7

TABLE OF CONTENTS

Preface

The Journey of Forgiveness deals with a fundamental aspect of human life—our need to forgive and be forgiven. As long as we are finite, relationships will be broken, trusts will be betrayed, and misunderstandings will lead to conflict. There will always be a need for forgiveness—and for books such as this which help us learn how best to forgive.

This resource can be used in a class setting as well as for individual study. Class teachers will want to take note of the goals and objectives provided at the beginning of each session. Also, some of the class activities require advance preparations. Teachers will want to review the activities in advance so that assignments can be made in class for the next week's session.

The Christian Education Commission wishes to thank Barbara Howard for her excellent work on this resource. Reconciliation is one of the basic ministries of the church. *The Journey of Forgiveness* is offered for use in the church in the belief that it will be an invaluable aid in that ministry.

Christian Education Commission

Introduction

One of our favorite family stories is about a race our daughter Joy ran when she was nearly seven. The day was unusually cold for fall in Missouri, and she had a cough. Knowing how involved children can get in competition, I reminded her, as she left the house with her father, "Be sure to keep your coat on, Joy." I just wanted her to be warm as she waited to run. Joy, who was particularly obedient as a child, thought I meant for her to keep it on all the time. So, as her Dad watched from the sidelines, she ran the entire race in her heavy, winter coat alongside all the children in their running outfits. Obviously, the heavy coat only interfered with her effort in the race.

I think of Joy in that race when I remember painful hurts I have carried as excess weight for long periods, when forgiveness would have lifted the burden of them. My journey has been easier the more I have been able to practice forgiving.

This book began, in some ways, in a class at Saint Paul School of Theology in 1976. My teacher, Jean Lambert, was working on her doctoral dissertation, and the class, "Divine Forgiveness—Human Resource," was helping her with her work. Jean's dissertation was published in book form in 1985, and I have used some of her insights in developing this resource. For chapter 5 I relied heavily on her material.

During the time I was in that class, I was also experiencing painful alienation from a dear friend. Jean's class was a life-changing experience for me. I wish I could say that after two or three months I was a bona fide forgiver.

But forgiving is a lifetime effort. My commitment to forgiveness began then. It continues. I believe forgiving is at the heart of the gospel. It is a source of life.

Throughout this material I have written about people who have taught me about forgiveness and nonforgiveness. They are disguised to protect their privacy. I have deliberately combined incidents so that no one is written about individually. But as I have recalled examples, I have discovered that there are universal attributes of freedom in the act of forgiving and of destruction in nonforgiveness. I continue to be taught by forgivers and nonforgivers.

Nonforgivers carry heavy loads of resentment, just as Joy carried her coat. I experience their cold distance. They do not enrich my life, but they teach me a great deal about the power of nonforgiveness to breed hatred and foster death.

There are many more people, though, who teach me about the power of forgiving. People in my family circle, my past, my present circle of friends, the early church, the scriptures, drama, literature, and in places I sometimes least expect to find them, model forgiving's liberating force.

My favorite recent story came to me through a speech at Williams College by Dr. Robert Coles, an American psychiatrist on the faculty of Havard University. It is the remarkable account of Ruby Bridges, one of the first black children to participate in school desegregation in New Orleans in the winter of 1960. Coles was in the Air Force, assigned in the southern part of the United States. Each day he watched six-year-old Ruby going into the school as mobs of people standing along the sidewalk cursed and spat on her. She was accompanied by two federal marshals, but people along the street were threatening to kill her. She walked into an empty building; the white people of her city had boycotted the school.

Each day Coles watched as Ruby seemingly talked to herself as she walked between rows of hostile, vicious people—most of them adults. Ruby seemed calm and assured. Coles found it difficult to believe that she was not experiencing horrible trauma. Finally, he decided to try to find out who she was talking to. He wanted to know what she was saying.

Ruby told the psychiatrist that she wasn't talking to the people. She was praying for them. Coles was amazed. He discovered that her parents had taught her that Christ, on the cross, had prayed for the people who crucified him. The very people who were rejecting and threatening Ruby were those for whom she had been taught to pray.

Coles saw a mystery going on in that setting that his academic training and all his medical knowledge could not explain. Ruby was living her faith.

I believe that Ruby Bridges' mental health was tied to her capacity to pray for her persecutors. To ask a child to experience what she was going through without faith in the power of forgiveness would be horrible. It was Ruby's faith that kept her free from trauma—her incredible conviction in the power of forgiveness.

I am grateful that Ruby journeyed ahead of me. Her courage to be forgiving in such circumstances gives me additional strength.

The truth of forgiveness is found in those who have drawn their maps, traveled their routes, and come through the difficult passages to the point where forgiving is like breathing. It is also found in those who keep struggling to comprehend its mysterious power.

One of my favorite hymns, "Help Us Accept Each Other," states that we can "know by heart, the table of forgiveness." Knowing by heart is to have something come automatically, spontaneously, readily. It is that kind of forgiveness I want to develop.

Some pilgrims have. They offer me hope for my journey. I hope this book will help you in your travels toward forgiveness.

Barbara Howard

MEDITATION

Liberating Prayer

I'm sorry for the times someone wasn't beautiful and I looked away.

I'm sorry for the times someone stretched out a hand and I pretended not to notice.

I'm sorry for the times someone needed to be held and I clung to safety instead.

I'm sorry for the times truth was on my tongue and I swallowed it instead of speaking it.

I'm sorry for the times love was in my heart and I was too embarrassed to express it.

I'm sorry for the times fear was in my heart and I didn't trust you with it.

I'm sorry for the times I claimed to be an innocent bystander and still I knew that by being a passive participant I was guilty for allowing wrong to be done.

I'm sorry for the times strangers asked me for something and I pretended not to realize what they needed.

I'm sorry for the times I haven't loved enough and the times I haven't loved with all of me.

I know you know I'm sorry, God, and I know you've already forgiven me.

Maybe that's why I'm not ashamed to say I'm sorry.
—Sharon and Thomas Neufer Emswiler[1]

Chapter 1

The Beginning of the Journey

Goals of this session:*
- To recognize the damage of unforgiveness
- To acknowledge forgiveness as the claim of God on the life of the Christian
- To affirm forgiveness as a journey of faith

Objectives:
- Participants will discuss unforgiveness as "living with death."
- The relationship of work and grace in forgiveness will be explored.
- Participants will consider that God's forgiveness is an unconditional gift, but that human forgiveness may be work as well as gift.
- Forgiveness as a journey will be illustrated with David Augsburger's model.
- The class members will have opportunity to critique their own journeys of forgiveness.

---

*Note to teacher: Class activities will require advance preparation. Assignments will need to be given to participants the week before each class session.

I had not seen my friend for nearly twenty years when we met in a supermarket. I was visiting friends in a small western town where my husband, Dick, and I had lived during the early years of our marriage. She had been our neighbor. We belonged to a Christian Bible study group, and our families became close friends. Her husband was the pastor of a Protestant church in our town. Mutual interest in scriptures, common values about family life, and shared humor were enough to build a good friendship. After our family moved back to the Midwest, she and I exchanged occasional letters and Christmas cards for the first couple of years. But, as sometimes happens, we gradually lost track of each other.

When we met, I was stunned at her appearance. She looked worn, ill, and tense. I asked about her family, and she related a stream of bitter, painful memories. Her husband had left her and their four children to marry one of his parishioners who had come to him for marital counseling. She poured out her story, filled with hostility. "I heard recently that he's sick," she snapped. "I hope he suffers. I hope he suffers a long time."

I could not believe the change in her. Years before she was joyful, outgoing, and compassionate. I thought the breakup in the relationship must have just happened, and that in time she would be able to deal with the rejection and betrayal to find a new base for her life. So I was dumbfounded when she told me that the divorce had taken place fifteen years before.

"I've done everything I can to let the kids know how rotten their father is, but they are easily fooled. Now that they are grown, I don't see them much, except for the youngest. He hates his father as much as I do. He just refuses to see his dad." She laughed bitterly. "You might say that he and I have a lot in common."

NONFORGIVENESS IS DESTRUCTIVE

My friend fits the description of a nonforgiver in Doris Donnelly's book, *Learning to Forgive*—a person led by anger, pain, or hatred. She has been directed by negative memories, does not act freely, tries to control situations and people, and is pressured by tension and stress. Nonforgivers are people who find their relationships with others strained, their relationship with God weakened, and who live with feelings of unrelieved guilt. A nonforgiver has little sense of self-worth. "Nonforgivers," Donnelly says, "live with death." They give up the possibility of future joy by holding on to the pain of the offense.[2]

My friend chose to allow the pain of her past to be her self-identity. She had not moved from the broken relationship with her husband, and was filled with bitter vindictiveness. Before we parted, she repeated her desire to see her former husband suffer. She no longer attended church because he had been permitted eventually to pastor another congregation in their denomination. She spoke of his present wife as "the harlot."

When we parted, I felt physically ill. I had never before seen such a clear example of "living death." My friend seemed intent on spending her time, energy, and resources in bitter retribution.

Donnelly offers some good counsel to those who stand in the same place as my friend:

When I refuse to forgive, I claim a triumph for failure—mine or another's. Someone's sin or mistake or error in judgment can lead our lives. Forgiveness, on the other hand, and most importantly, is an invitation to redeem failure. Guilt as a healthy feeling is probably alerting me to a failure somewhere that needs resolving. There are those who tell us that all guilt is useless and unnecessary. This is simply not so. Guilt as a healthy feeling begs for acknowledgment and resolution through self-forgiveness or by forgiving others their trespasses. To do otherwise is to choose to live without accepting failure as part of life and without growing because of it. It is to live haunted, if not consumed, by a guilt that leaves all my relationships, including the one I have with myself in a debit column.[3]

My friend was "haunted. . .consumed" by her past. She had kept that past alive for fifteen years and refused to live in the present or move into the future. While the past cannot be changed, it can be redeemed. The promise to the Christian is sure: "When anyone is united to Christ, there is a new world; the old order has gone, and a new order has already begun."[4] "It is all the doing of God who has reconciled me through Christ and has permitted me to be a minister of reconciliation."[5]

Christian forgiveness is a way of bringing to destructive events new and creative possibilities. To discover the power of forgiveness is to find that freedom to do away with "old things." It is also to determine to live in the present moment with hope for a future. Nonforgivers are bound to a past which decides how each day is lived.

Many students of forgiveness—ministers, counselors, therapists—believe there is a strong connection between mental health and the capacity to forgive. Emotionally healthy people are not afraid of the future: they experience the present and enjoy the past. To live in or to deny the past is to cut out a significant part of one's experience. Forgiveness provides a context where there is freedom to see things as they are and have been.

Forgiveness is not just a matter of "balancing books in a ledger." Forgiving is a process, rather than a single event. Forgivers are engaged in a lifetime commitment to a relationship. There are many forms of forgiving, but each one involves some struggle, often pain, time, effort, communication.

In some communities of faith, the emphasis has been on the "gift" of forgiveness. God's grace, which is gift and enables our forgiveness, is held up as the human model. The story of Jesus on the cross, and his plea, "Forgive them; they know not what they do," are used to illustrate the nature of forgiveness as grace. When forgiveness as gift is distorted, the pain of the wounded person can be glossed over, and the person experiences what David Augsburger terms "false forgiveness."

FALSE FORGIVENESS

Such artificial forgiving creates a facade in a relationship where persons are unable to be honest about the pain of the breach. This is neither redemptive to the person who acted inappropriately nor helpful to the person who was hurt. The gift of forgiveness rests in God's grace, and human forgiveness begins with that recognition. It is important, however, to remember that we are not God, and therefore the gift of forgiveness enables us to engage in the process of communication and restoration with confidence that both parties can be healed. The burden of forgiving rests on all who are involved in the break.

In settings where works are strongly emphasized, repentance must precede forgiveness. Often scriptures from James are used to support this position. The tension between grace and works is evident in the story of Rahab in Joshua 2–6. This account is referred to in James 2:24 as support for the statement, "Faith without works is dead" (2:25 IV).

It is important for us as Christians to accept God's forgiveness. We are called to be agents of God's reconciliation. But the ministry of reconciliation is more than gift. It also involves work. Therefore we can appropriately paraphrase James 2:25 and say, "Forgiveness without works is not forgiveness." The grace of forgiveness makes possible the works of forgiveness, however. God's unconditional love enables us to confront our worst selves, accept that we are forgiven, and forgive others. This work is never ending and becomes a way of life for the practicing forgiver.

TWO ASPECTS OF FORGIVENESS

The difficulty, though, is that there is no formula for forgiving. An X number of deeds combined with Y understanding of grace may not necessarily equal forgiveness. Each person must determine the way the process will begin, how it will continue, and if it will become a lifestyle.

There are two significant aspects of forgiveness. Self-forgiveness frees one from guilt and painful memories even when others refuse to participate in the healing action. Mutual forgiveness heals broken relationships and restores community. These two facets of forgiving allow creative, continuing growth.

Self-forgiveness is essential. People like my friend in the supermarket, who refuse to accept any responsibility for the fractured relationship, begin to loathe themselves and their world. When accusation and blame are put aside, there is a climate for forgiving oneself and another.

W. H. Auden, in "As I Walked Out One Evening," wrote, "Thou shalt love thy crooked neighbor with thy crooked heart."[6] No one is perfect—a "crooked heart" describes everyone. Consequently, when someone is offended, it becomes necessary to look at the offender as another hurting human being rather than as the enemy.

Despite protestations to the contrary, most people who refuse to forgive probably feel that they themselves are unforgivable. They refuse then to acknowledge their part in the alienation.

In turn, people suffer deeply if they are closed out of relationships because of their actions. The scriptural story of Rahab was mentioned earlier. The following essay illustrates the pain suffered by one who is excluded from her community's healing forgiveness.

"Rahab, I'd Like to Talk to You"

Rahab, did they ever let you forget? Even as a harlot you knew who God was. You recognized the nation Israel as God's people and you sheltered their spies. You are one of four women mentioned in Christ's lineage. The Bible tells us many things, but there is something it does not tell us. . . .

I need to know this. I need to know how to overcome my past, the deeds that eventually led to a police record. . . . How did you do it, Rahab? Were you ever able to shake off that title, "the harlot"? I am comforted that Matthew writes, ". . . and to Salmon was born Boaz by Rahab . . ." and there is no title attached to your name. God did forgive and forget. . . . We, you and I, Rahab, are of this earthly world, and people do not forget. Many do not even forgive. Did you also walk in the despair of your past with violet shadows growing darker under your eyes from sleepless nights? Nights spent wishing you could erase the past but to no avail? I wonder this too, Rahab, when you went to worship with fellow believers, did the people rejoice at your presence? Or did the mothers keep a close watch over their sons in case you might get too close? Did they ever really forget?

I think that perhaps they did not forget. I think probably you were often shunned. My throat feels tight and my eyes brim with tears as I think of it. I am also shunned. I know how it feels to be avoided in order to prevent contamination. I want to cry out, "But you don't understand. God has washed away all that filth. I am clean." If anyone hears my silent plea, I never seem to see a sign of it. It hurts me so. What did you do, Rahab? Did you hold your head high and walk undaunted amongst them? Or did you hide away and seldom go out? It must have been hard for you. God has forgiven us, Rahab. He has given us a new life and the "old has passed away." I wish that other believers would recognize that. I wish they weren't so cold.

Did rebellion well up inside you when you heard your title "the harlot"? My soul rebels and I want to break free from this mold I am put in. My heart weeps, "The past is dead, let's leave it buried." No one hears me. . . . God honored your faith, so I feel you must have stayed steadfast. The opposition you had must have made you strong in your faith. Give me the words of God, Rahab, the words that enabled you to live with your past. . . .

My only hope is to find my rest in the forgiveness of God. I am forgiven and someday the world around me will know that. When I die and am received into our heavenly paradise, I will search you out and hold your hand. We will talk and laugh and understand each other. Like you I will at last be completely free from my past. In heaven's glory. . . my heart will be free to find joy in my salvation because my past will finally have been erased. For all time.[7]

This woman's story is tragic. The promise inherent in the body of Christ is that people find meaning, forgiveness, and hope in life on earth. The promise of a "heavenly reward" is not enough. The church community this author protects with her anonymity (she uses a pen name in order to protect family, friends, and her home church) suffers the "living death" of unforgiveness. Often promiscuous sexual behavior or some other behavior becomes the "sin" which seems the most important focus of some groups.

Much of the preaching and energy of the people is given to judging the behavior of others. Right behavior is often seen as what is not done, rather than as acts of loving compassion. Punishment is emphasized in such a setting. Sometimes damaging "shunning" practices are used as a means of control.

The church, as the body of Christ, is called to restoration—of relationships, of people, of humanizing structures. The church, and those who live the gospel, provide an opportunity for people to recognize the claim of God on their lives. That claim includes forgiveness.

REPENTANCE AND FORGIVENESS

In the earliest days of the Restoration movement there was strong emphasis on repentance. "Cry repentance to this generation" is a familiar phrase in early church literature. The need for repentance continues and is nowhere more needed than in an unforgiving heart. Some demand repentance before forgiveness; others believe that forgiveness precedes the capacity to repent. Geoffrey Spencer points to the essential nature of both:

The church lives out of a perspective that considers sin with utmost seriousness, and embraces forgiveness with supreme confidence. The experience of forgiveness is inevitably social. Apart from a community exhibiting the fruits of forgiveness, the concept lacks body and substance, hence persuasiveness. God's forgiveness is only credible where men and women live creatively out of the conviction of having been forgiven, and where forgiveness is actively and intentionally practiced.[8]

Spencer says we experience the forgiveness of God as it takes place in our own lives. The cross of Christ offers to believers the claim of God's forgiveness. Despite all that we are, have been, or ever will be, God has interceded for us. As Paul writes, "God commendeth his love toward us, in that while we were yet sinners, Christ died for us" (Rom. 5:8). But as is evidenced in the account, "Rahab, I'd like to talk to you," God's forgiveness is understood in human relationships. People desperately need to feel accepted. The promise of "heavenly communion" is inadequate. The church community makes God's forgiveness "credible."

Such credibility is not expressed in theories, doctrines, or philosophical positions. It is understood when we do something hurtful, cruel, or wrong, and the offense is met with forgiveness that frees us to change the consequences of our actions. Forgiveness is believable when we are wounded by another and are able to embrace the offender and create a new future together.

MOVING TOWARD FORGIVENESS

Forgiveness is not a magical potion which automatically removes the hurt and returns everything to its original place. The claim of forgiveness is God's promise that while nothing stays the same there is a trustworthy source of support offering redemptive power to the forgiver. To believe in forgiveness is to live by such a promise.

Many people use forgiveness and love interchangeably. Certainly one cannot forgive without love, but neither can one love without forgiveness. They are, however, not synonymous. Loving is the foundation and the force in forgiving. Without it, there can be no relationship. The word *forgiveness* is a form of the verb *to give*. It is experienced as gift, also.

David Augsburger calls forgiveness the final form of love and uses the following chart to illustrate some steps that are necessary in the work of forgiving.[9]

Forgiveness is
the final form of love

Step 1. To see the other as having worth again, regardless of wrongdoing

Is this forgiveness? No, it is the prerequisite love.

—————————VALUING————————→

Step 2. To see the other as equally precious again, in spite of the pain felt

Is this then forgiveness? No, it is the requisite first step.

—————————LOVING————————→

Step 3. To cancel demands on the past, recognizing that changing the unchangeable is impossible

Is this forgiveness? No, this is coming to terms with reality. No, it is the reality which undergirds it.

—————————CANCELING DEMANDS—→

Step 4. To work through the anger and pain felt by both in reciprocal trusting and risking until genuineness in intention is perceived and repentance is seen by both to be authentic

Is this forgiveness? Yes, forgiving is now being done.

—————————TRUSTING NOW————————→

Step 5. To drop the demands for an ironclad guarantee of future behavior and open the future to choice, to spontaneity, to the freedom to fail again.

Is this forgiveness? Yes, this is the central work of forgiving.

—————————OPENING THE FUTURE—→

Step 6. To touch each other deeply, to feel moved in warmth, love, compassion, to celebrate it in mutual recognition that right relationships have been achieved.

And this? This is the bonding, celebrating.

—————————CELEBRATING LOVE—→

Augsburger's chart is one map of the journey of for-giveness. His model describes the first step as a will-ingness to view the person who wronged us as a being of infinite worth, regardless of what has hap-pened. We begin to establish a new relationship with a commitment to the value of that person who hurt us. For some, this is the most difficult step. Having been wronged, betrayed, overlooked, rejected—or what-ever the negative experience—now we are called to look at the other as a person of infinite worth.

The second step is to reaffirm love. We do that when we cease to be neutral about the person. We not only value the individual, but the source of our grief becomes precious to us again. We see beyond our own hurt and allow ourselves to experience the love that bound us before the alienation.

A JOURNEY OF MANY STEPS

Sometimes people try to move from alienation to reconciliation in one giant leap—which is why fester-ing bitterness may continue. Forgiveness is usually a journey of many steps. Once we allow ourselves to see the person or persons from whom we have been separated as having value, we can cancel demands. For instance, if the approach to our difficulty is to say, "You can be forgiven if..." we have not begun the journey. There may be a strong desire for guaran-tees, but human relationships do not offer such a luxury. To begin the journey is to confront and ac-cept the broken relationship as real.

The past is done; it cannot be undone. It cannot be erased; it happened. A common human lament is, "If only I could do that over again," or "If only I had not done..." Marianne is an example of someone who struggled with this principle:

Marianne lived in the "if only" stage for several years. One afternoon she was in a hurry to get to school to pick up Tim for his music lessons. The baby was in the backyard, and Marianne had made arrangements with the neighbor to care for her. She rushed into the garage, opened the door with the automatic device, and backed her car out over her two-year-old child seated in the driveway.

The neighbor, in the meantime, was waiting in the backyard for Marianne to bring her the child. There had been a communication mix-up and the result was a horrible tragedy. Over and over again, Marianne created different scenarios. But nothing could change the event. The child was dead.

The work of forgiveness had to begin for both women. The need to accept the events of the past, to recognize them as unchangeable, is one step in the journey.

Some people seem unable to stop trying to rewrite the past. It is over, and all that can be changed about it is how it is used. If the past is not used, we are unable to live in the present or lean toward the future. But the past begins to be useful when we start trusting again.

This requires mutuality, not blind trust. When the prodigal son returned home, he trusted his father. He recognized that he had no rights, but he knew he had a place to go. The father trusted his son and ran down the path to greet him. The son could have been there to ask for more money, but the movement of repentance was in both parties. This was the result of mutual trust.

LEARNING TO TRUST

The original meanings of the word *trust* are from a ninth-century Scandinavian egalitarian culture: "To comfort, to console, to confide in." If I have wronged another, and forgiveness is in motion, I want to share the hurt that prompted the wrong. I want also to ex-

27

press my sorrow at my actions and comfort the one I hurt. Reciprocity is vital in the forgiving journey. The offender must be willing to claim the hurtful behavior. The one who has been hurt must be willing to acknowledge the pain and move beyond it. "I'll forgive her, but I'll never trust her again," is another way of saying, "I will not forgive her."

CREATING A NEW FUTURE

Reciprocal trust creates a new future. It opens the door to spontaneity and freedom to fail again. Without this, there can be no "bonding, celebrating love" that is the goal of the journey. Jane and Jim found such a new future:

Jane and Jim celebrated their fiftieth anniversary. They shared with friends the joys and sorrows of their past. In a small dinner meeting, they spoke of years of learning and relearning trust. They tearfully recalled the death of their teenage daughter in a horrible car accident, of Jim's mother's lingering illness after a stroke, of Jim's forced "early retirement" from his company. Jane spoke first: "There were times in our marriage when we hardly knew each other. The distance between us was like a desert."

Then Jim described his withdrawal from friends, former working companions, church activities, and Jane hesitatingly shared the pain of a "short-term affair."

The friends listened quietly as Jim said, "I thought our marriage was over, but I can honestly say that I trust Jane more deeply than I ever have in my life."

Jane spoke again: "I believe that forgiveness is the most powerful force on the face of the earth. It is possible only through the power of love."

Such events are not science fiction or fairy tales. They are the stories of flesh and blood people who sit beside us and live next door. The life-giving force of forgiveness continues wherever people respond to the power of the Holy Spirit to restore, renew, resurrect.

The journey of forgiveness is primarily the pilgrimage of dynamic love. It is the sojourn of people willing to suffer with and for each other. The Augsburger chart is only one model. There are probably as many maps as there are forgivers. Perhaps the most creative key to the journey is found in the life of Christ. Christ left us a treasure map of intense struggle, pain, joy, and peace, where the place of arrival is richer than our imaginings.

In the final pages of *The Last Battle,* the conclusion of "The Chronicles of Narnia" by C. S. Lewis, the land of Narnia is opened to the followers of the lion, Aslan (the Christ figure). As they move into this new dimension, Lucy speaks to the fawn, Tumnus, about the new unfolding world about her. Tumnus assures her that

"the further up and further in you go, the bigger everything gets. The inside is larger than the outside"...

"I see," she said. "This is still Narnia, and more real and more beautiful than the Narnia.... outside.... world within world, Narnia within Narnia."

"Yes," said Mr. Tumnus, "Like an onion, except that as you continue to go in and in, each circle is larger than the last."[10]

Narnia is Lewis' metaphor for the kingdom of God. It is a new place, but it isn't just in some ethereal realm. The children in the story find its reality in their own adventures. It is a new land each time it is discovered.

Like Narnia, forgiveness is a new land each time we discover it. It is imploring us to find its beauty. It is the new terrain that is with us in this world, in our everyday experience, if we are willing to start the journey.

Activities

1. Recall the story of the "friend in the super-market." Have the class respond to Doris Don-nelly's description of nonforgiveness as "living death." Ask people to finish the statement, "If I were that woman, I would..."

2. What work of forgiveness could be enacted by the friend in the supermarket that might start her on a journey to forgiveness? List four specific actions.

3. Ask three people to each speak three minutes about one of the following:
   a. God's forgiveness is assured in Christ.
   b. Human forgiveness is an act of repentance.
   c. Repentance is a response to divine forgive-ness.

4. A week before this class, assign someone to read the account of Rahab described in Joshua, begin-ning with the second chapter and continuing through 6:27. Ask another class member to read the material in the lesson, "Rahab, I'd like to talk to you." Give a few minutes for each person to report on the material, highlighting the stories. Ask the class then to respond to the scripture in James 2:25. In what ways could this scripture apply to the person who has been branded and is living in nonforgiveness?

5. Place the David Augsburger chart on a black-board or overhead projector. Have class members determine where they are on their for-giveness journey. (It is not necessary for people to share the events that they are working through, but this may be done if they wish.)

6. End the class by singing the hymn, "Forgive Our Sins as We Forgive," HS 108.

NOTES

1. Sharon and Thomas Neufer Emswiler, *Women and Worship: A Guide to Non-Sexist Hymns, Prayers, and Liturgies* (San Francisco: Harper & Row, 1980), 56–57. Copyright © 1974 by Sharon and Thomas Neufer Emswiler. Reprinted by permission of Harper and Row, Publishers, Inc.
2. Doris Donnelly, *Learning to Forgive* (New York: Macmillan Publishing Company, 1979), 30–57. Copyright © 1979 by Doris Donnelly. Reprinted with permission of the publisher.
3. Ibid., 55.
4. II Corinthians 5:17 NEB.
5. II Corinthians 5:18 Moffatt.
6. W. H. Auden, "As I Walked Out One Evening," *Another Time* (New York: Random House, 1940), 26.
7. Elizabeth Wiebe, "Rahab, I'd Like to Talk to You," *The Mennonite* (July 3, 1984): 336. Used by permission.
8. Geoffrey Spencer, *Strangers and Pilgrims* (Independence, Missouri: Herald House, 1984), 96.
9. David Augsburger, *Caring Enough to Forgive/Caring Enough to Not Forgive* (Ventura, California: Regal Books, 1981), 31. © Copyright 1981. Used by permission.
10. C. S. Lewis, *The Last Battle* (New York: Macmillan Publishing Company, 1962), 170–171.

MEDITATION

some things I can't forgive

You will recognize these sins, Lord.
You have forgiven them before—
Not sins committed and redone—
But the very sins you once forgave.

By withholding self-forgiveness,
I kept a grip upon these sins
And fed and nurtured proud old guilts
Till they grew strong and bred new sins.

There are some things I can't forgive.
I've got higher standards than you do,
And tougher standards still for friends.
I judge myself against them both.

Lord, help me to enlarge my heart,
To stretch and make room to receive
Your Holy Spirit who forgives
And who alone makes possible
Acceptance of forgiveness.

—**Michael Becker**[1]

Chapter 2

Self-forgiveness—A Beginning Step

Goals of this session:*
- To consider the value of self-forgiveness
- To acknowledge the role of guilt as impediment to self-forgiveness
- To see the relationship between grace, self-acceptance, and self-forgiveness

Objectives:
- Participants will discuss the concepts of grace, self-acceptance, and self-forgiveness.
- Transformation rather than endurance will be defined as the goal of forgiveness.
- The "centered self" and a definition of self-centeredness will be explored.
- Participants will assess their own sense of self-worth.

---

*Note to teacher: Class activities will require advance preparation. Assignments will need to be given to participants the week before each class session.

One of the ideals of Christianity is that we love everybody. The divine imperative in John, "God so loved the world," sets the model for Christian relationships. Divine love is unceasing, unconditional, and unrelenting. God reconciles us in Christ Jesus; the Cross symbolizes the restoration of that divine/ human relationship.

Christians often espouse a universal love, but in reality there are people in the Christian community who are not permitted to interact. Sometimes the break is so severe that a relationship is not possible. For the person who desires forgiveness, the journey may begin here with the self. The following story is an illustration of this principle:

Where Was God?—A Journey of Healing

By Louise Garrison

This has been written in tears: Tears of a 4-year-old who doesn't understand what Daddy is doing. Tears of a 6-year-old who is told, "It won't hurt much longer." Tears of an 8-year-old who is told, "Stop crying, it doesn't hurt any more," or "If you don't stop crying, I'll give you something to cry about." Tears of a 10-year-old who hears, "If you don't do this to help me, I'll leave; and then you, your mother, and your brother will have no food or place to live." Tears of a 12-year-old girl who prays that God won't make her pregnant (and prays that prayer for seven more years). Tears of a 14-year-old who prays that God will wipe her father off the earth.

Incest is the subject I have more knowledge of than any other. It is also the subject that is the most difficult to write about. By so doing, I leave myself exposed, stripped of all pretenses of who or what I am, and therefore, totally vulnerable. But so vividly do I remember the abuse, so strongly do I understand the need to be affirmed as a child of God, and so powerfully am I moved by the Spirit of God, that I am persuaded to bring light to a crime that must be an abomination unto God.. . .

As a parent, I do everything in my power to protect my son from fearful situations. I suspect other parents do likewise.

But fear is a state of being that an abused child knows intimately. An abused child lives in fear created by someone who professes to love him or her.

Eventually the child grows to adulthood, as I have, afraid of life and suspicious of other people. It came as a shock to realize I was terrified of men and that I must constantly battle this fear.

I learned from my experiences that I am not lovable. If the person hurting me was supposed to love me and continued to hurt me something must be wrong with me that made me unlovable. A child cannot draw any other conclusion.

I don't recall the day I recognized this or even remember consciously taking ownership of the thought, but I know it is part of me that I work daily to erase. No matter how hard I tried to please my father, nothing I could do satisfied him except relieving his insatiable sexual appetite. That left me in a constant state of fear.

We are taught early in our Christian education that our bodies are the temples of Christ. But my temple had been violated so many times it ceased to have any significance to me except as an object of hate. I was raped more than 400 times in my childhood and adolescent years. The memories of those experiences are horrifying.

During that time, my body was the source of nothing but grief and pain. It was demeaned to the point where I saw it. . . only as the prison of my soul.

I was desperate to control what was happening to me, but I couldn't. Nothing belonged to me. Nothing was sacred, and I had absolutely no rights or privacy. So as a child, I learned to control the one thing I could—my emotions.

During my mid-teens, however, another contributor to my self-hatred developed. I found my body responding physically. Not understanding how I could enjoy something I hated so much, I concluded that I was evil. "Good" people didn't do this awful thing.

I believed everyone could ask for and receive forgiveness from God, but came to think I was the exception. All persons except me were entitled to God's mercies. That belief has imprisoned me for years, and only recently have I been able to verbalize that I believed I was not part of God's kingdom.

There was a time when I did not care if I lived or died. Death held promise because that was where all the wrongs would be righted. The emotional pain of everyday life would find release. Therefore, death was not frightening. Only life was.

I finally shut the door to my feelings, and became a person who did not live, but merely existed. Survival was the key, and I refined survival to an art.

I pretended to hide inside my body. In my mind, I left the rape experiences completely. I knew he was not doing anything to the real me because I had retreated into that inner part of my being that was sacred, clean, and pure. He didn't know that part of me existed, so he couldn't rape that part of me. . . .

What has happened is that I have sought to hide the only part of me that is truly mine—my inner being. It is the only aspect of my existence that has not been dredged out, knocked around, beaten, and demeaned. My inner being belongs to me. It is sacred territory.

I wear armor and create soldiers to protect myself. The armor is my masks, and the soldiers are the different roles I play when I'm performing on the stage of life. I play the roles brilliantly, and my soldiers protect me.

I have just begun to take the masks off, but they have been on so long that the stage make-up is caked. I have found it very painful to peel the layers off, but I am determined to succeed.

A voice calls to me, and it gives me no peace. It keeps urging me forward even through the pain. It is the persistent and persuasive voice that transforms the world and transcends its pain and suffering. It is the voice of the one who has borne all our grief and suffered all of life's indignities. It is the voice of the God who came to us incarnate in Jesus Christ. It speaks of the healing relationship and the relationship in healing.

Claiming my innocence was painful. In so doing I had to decree that my father was unworthy of my love. But more painful is the knowledge that he did not love me. I fought accepting that knowledge for so many years. It was easier to believe I was evil than to believe my father did not love me. But as long as I chose to deny it, freedom was impossible.

Where was God when I needed God most? I have searched my soul into its depths for the answer, and in that search I have found a new freedom that comes from experiencing God—a God who comes to us in whatever form we need and in whatever place we happen to be.

This very question is our common denominator. It is the question we ask where there is no more light at the end of the tunnel. The question plagues us when we are in crisis. Each of us struggles with this question from the time we are able to identify what the word "God" images for us.

I have found my answer. My answer came from the crucified Christ as he cried out in his passion from the cross, "*Eloi, Eloi, lama sabachthani?*"

"My God, my God, why has thou forsaken me?" Surely a God who has such mercy and such love would not let a son die on a cross, even if we are sinners. I, a mere mortal with limited capabilities for love, would move heaven and earth and fight with all my being for the life of my son. If God's love is greater than ours, why wasn't the son saved?

Scripture tells us in Matthew 27:40 that the chief priests, lawyers, and elders asked the same question. Even the bandits who were crucified with him taunted him in the same way. Jesus died a broken man—mocked by his accusers, betrayed by his disciples, and denied by one of his closest friends. Jeered at, spit at, taunted, ridiculed, laughed at. But God had the last word, because Jesus overcame every earthly affliction. No matter what the abuse, the message God has given us in the resurrection is that coercive power never works; it only destroys. God has the final word, and that word is Life.

Victims of coercive power can find salvation and redemption in the message of the cross. The message is not only that Christ died for our sins but that Christ died because of sin. That sin is the need for one person to render another a slave. The need to control, the need to hold power over someone else is, I believe, the reason people abuse children. Who better is there to exert power over than a helpless child?

But Jesus' death is our resurrection. If there were ever a time when God could have used coercive power, it was on that day when the earth shook and the sky was dark and Jesus was nailed to a cross. But instead God raised Jesus from the dead. And just as God raised Jesus from the dead, God has also raised me from my death. I believe God did not remove me miraculously from my surroundings because God knows that coercive power never works.

You and I are children of God and can receive that same love from God as Jesus did. That love will bring me to the light at the end of my tunnel, and that love will bring you to the light at the end of your tunnel.

God the father. Can I really love God the Father? If my own father was my molester, can anyone including God expect that I could love Him with all my heart and soul? Is it possible to love someone, something, or some other if the image is a reminder of my own father?

My God is the creator, sustainer, and redeemer of all life. Some say God is the Father. Others say God is Mother or Spirit. The important message is that God will speak to us in our own imagery.

It is not important whether we believe in God the Father, or God the Mother, or God the Spirit, or God the Other. What is important is that we allow ourselves to hear God speak to us in ways that will make our lives whole and complete. I believe God—whoever or whatever God is—will move in our lives with such force that we will be carried to new freedom and life, if only we will be open to the opportunity.[2]

One of the striking statements in this testimony, "It was easier to believe I was evil than to believe my father did not love me," is a clue to the struggle of self-forgiveness. Garrison continues to describe the need to make the first step: "As long as I chose to deny it, freedom was impossible."

Louise Garrison's story is tragic. It is, however, the history she must embrace. Self-forgiveness enables her to accept God's love which becomes real to her in the experience of self-acceptance. For as she so eloquently describes, "new freedom and life" await her acceptance. This is the promise of the gospel.

Some distort the gospel by believing that the Christian's only option is to endure suffering. Jesus Christ offers the power of *transformation,* not merely *endurance.* While some Christians continue to emphasize passive forgiveness and the endurance of violence as a form of forgiveness, the Crucifixion and Resurrection are God's proclamation that transformation is at the heart of the message of Jesus Christ. The hideous suffering of the Cross illustrates the suffering of all humanity, but Resurrection is the Word of transformation. Self-forgiveness is a willingness to accept that Word.

One roadblock to self-forgiveness is blaming— oneself or the other. Blaming keeps an offender categorized, thus prohibiting mutuality. Blaming keeps the offense alive. The event, rather than the person, must be the focus of redemptive anger. Reconciliation with oneself means to refuse to continue to be victimized, to acknowledge the injury, and to work for justice as a redemptive activity.

A destructive past can be redeemed only by forgiveness. Hannah Arendt describes forgiving as "the only reaction that does not merely react but acts anew and unexpectedly, unconditioned by the act that provoked it and therefore freeing from its consequences both the one who forgives and the one who is forgiven."[3] Ultimately, the most horrible history can be transformed only by remembering, by facing it, by acknowledging its effects, and then by using it creatively to set in motion the power of forgiveness.

Forgiveness, then, starts with the person who has been hurt, wronged, or treated unjustly. Before forgiving can begin, if I am the injured one, I must recognize and cherish my own value. Otherwise, I will define myself by the injury. I must recognize that whatever demeans me demeans God, for I am God's creation. If I value the presence of the Holy Spirit in whom I "live and move and have [my] being" (Acts 17:28), then I am able to take responsibility for my life despite the act of injustice against me.

To live in the context of forgiveness, to embrace past hurts and be liberated from their damaging effects, is self-acceptance. Carl Jung, the great psychiatrist, considered self-acceptance "the essence of the moral problem and the epitome of a whole outlook on life."[4] It is the key to emotional health and demands honesty and self-forgiving.

In *The Road Less Traveled*, Scott Peck describes disabled personality types: the neurotic and the character disordered. Neurotic people, Peck states, assume too much responsibility for problems in a relationship. "It is all my fault," a neurotic will think. Character-disordered people automatically assume that anything wrong is someone else's fault. For emotional health, both types need to learn to be responsible—first to themselves and then to others. Both reflect low self-esteem.[5]

If Louise Garrison had continued to blame herself for her abuse, she would have remained neurotic. If she had failed to recognize her own value and had continued to see herself as "victim" she would have remained character disordered. To achieve emotional health, Louise has discovered a way to acknowledge her painful history and move beyond it. She is learning to feel again—to risk vulnerability. She is learning to love herself and is becoming whole.

BECOMING A CENTERED SELF

For centuries Western Christianity emphasized self-denial, self-sacrifice, and self-denunciation. The expression "self-centered" held (and continues to hold, in some traditions) negative connotations. But a centered self is one which senses the divine power within. A centered self accepts God's unconditional love as gift. The Judeo-Christian cornerstone of self-acceptance is "thou shalt love thy neighbor as thyself." In the Golden Rule, "Do unto others as you would have them do unto you," the self also sets the standard of one's conduct toward others.

Jesus lived a life that was fully centered. Christ, consequently, represents what it means to be wholly self-giving, the offering of a self-aware person. In the fourth chapter of John the gospel writer tells a story which illustrates this principle. Jesus was passing through Samaria when he came to the well at Sychar. Weary, he stopped to rest. It was midday. The women usually came to the well in the early morning to get water for the day, and perhaps again in the late evening. A woman from the village approached the well and Jesus asked her for a drink. The woman recognized that Jesus was a Jew. She expressed surprise at his willingness even to speak to her, much less to ask for a drink.

At that point, Jesus began a conversation with her in which he told her of God's free gift—"living water" from a well so deep that those who drink of it "do not thirst again." It was, Jesus declared, "a well of water springing up into everlasting life." The woman asked for such water, and Jesus described her to herself. There were no secrets she could hide behind now. God desires to be worshiped "in spirit and in truth." Confronted with the truth of herself, in the presence of God incarnate in Christ Jesus, the woman recognized her value. She hastened back to her village with new insights and a new question, "Is not this the Christ?"[6]

For John Newton, the former slave trader, the theme of his life—on discovering God's love in the midst of his own sin—was "amazing grace...I once was lost, but now I'm found." Scott Peck agrees:

Once we perceive the reality of grace, our understanding of ourselves as meaningless and insignificant is shattered. The fact that there exists beyond ourselves and our conscious will a powerful force that nurtures our growth and evolution is enough to turn our notions of self-insignificance topsy-turvy.[7]

Guilt may be the major impediment to a sense of self-worth. While guilt is initially a healthy reminder that something is out of harmony in our spiritual lives, if held close as a prized possession it shackles our behavior. God's grace expressed in Christ Jesus frees us from guilt. To hold on to it is a denial of the gift in Christ.

This is the meaning of the Lord's Supper: the gracious forgiveness of our sins. If we took the experience of the sacrament of the Lord's Supper seriously, we would realize that no one holds on to our sins but ourselves. Loving ourselves and accepting our imperfection is the beginning of true repentance, for repentance is rooted in an awareness of our limitations. This understanding is essential in relationships and vital to emotional well-being as Martha discovered.

Martha promised her mother that she would never have to go to a rest home. "No matter what, Mom, I'll always take care of you." Her mother contracted Alzheimer's disease, and finally when Martha was unable to care for her, she placed her in a home. The mother, as do many victims of the disease, became verbally abusive and condemning. Martha was consumed with guilt.

Martha could find comfort in the wise words of Madeleine L'Engle, given to a friend in a similar situation. "I don't think real guilt is ever much of a problem for us. It's false guilt that causes the trouble."[8]

FALSE GUILT DISABLES

All of us at some time or another experience guilt, but we often have those feelings about the wrong things. When we confront our guilts readily—when we are honest about the reasons for our guilt—then we can act appropriately and responsibly. Our desire to protect ourselves from our own brokenness causes us to develop attitudes of false forgiveness.

False guilt is the twinge we have when we do something hurtful, and berate ourselves, only to continue repeating the behavior. False guilt is also the inability to accept our own mistakes and to take responsibility for them. False guilt is to claim perfection for ourselves and then, when we are unable to be perfect, to condemn ourselves. When we play God, we are plagued with false guilt.

SELF-FORGIVENESS IS ESSENTIAL
Martha's mother can no longer be cared for at home. She requires the professional staff of a long-term health care facility. Martha is not God. She can neither remove the illness from her mother, nor be held responsible for it. She can find her own center and see herself as cherished by God. She can value that which she gives her mother as her offering of that self.

Many times we ignore the self, believing that the object of our pilgrimage is to find God. In our search for God, we often disregard the guide set forth in the first epistle of John: "No one has ever seen God; but as long as we love one another God will live in us."[9]

Self-forgiveness is necessary in order to love others. We can accept God's grace and take the first step on our journey to a life-style of forgiveness. We can claim ourselves as worthy and loved by our Creator.

Activities

1. The week before the session ask a member of the class to read Louise Garrison's story and bring a report to the class. Give five minutes for people to write down "feeling" words (anger, sorrow, frustration) as a response. Allow time for discussion.

2. Using a sheet of paper, create a scale. Balance on the scale "qualities that I cherish in myself" / "qualities I find hard to forgive."

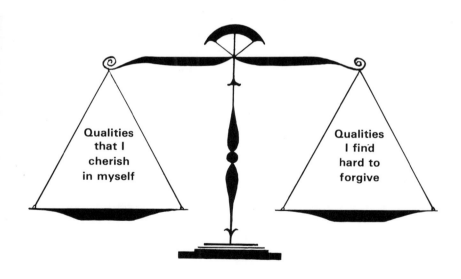

3. Using Scott Peck's definition of neurotic and character disordered, invite each participant to de-

termine which of the characteristics might be self-descriptive. A blackboard illustration of a continuum of the two extremes might be used, with the class members placing themselves on the continuum. (Emphasize that this is an individual, private exercise.) What is needed for self-love?

4. Divide the group into pairs. Have one person speak to another, "Once when I failed to _____, I felt _____." Allow time for each person to respond to the other. Then ask each partner to say to the other, "I believe I am forgiven and loved of God." This exercise is designed to help participants express self-forgiveness.

5. Process this activity. In groups of five or six, have participants discuss their response to the exercise.

6. Dr. Gerald Jampolsky in *Goodbye to Guilt* observes that "holding on to guilt is guaranteed to (1) make us feel under attack; (2) justify our feelings of anger toward ourself or someone else; (3) destroy our self-esteem and confidence; (4) make us feel depressed, hollow, and empty; (5) destroy our sense of peace; (6) make us feel unloved."[10] Because it is unlikely that anyone would choose to experience any of the six, what are some reasons why people do? Have a panel of six discuss each of the preceding guarantees and how forgiveness can release people from these dilemmas.

7. Write a letter of forgiveness to yourselves for something you have done that caused you guilt or remorse.

8. End the session by singing together, "If by Your Grace I Choose to Be," *HS* 432.

NOTES

1. Michael Becker, *alive now!* (May/June 1979): 54. Copyright © 1979 *The Upper Room;* used by permission.
2. Louise Garrison, "Where Was God?—A Journey of Healing," *Sojourners,* 13, no. 10 (November 1984): 23. Reprinted with permission from *Sojourners,* Box 29272, Washington, D.C. 20017.
3. Hannah Arendt, *The Human Condition* (Chicago: University of Chicago Press, 1970), 241.
4. Carl Jung, *Modern Man in Search of a Soul* (New York: Harcourt, Brace & Co., 1955), 235.
5. Scott Peck, *The Road Less Traveled* (New York: Simon and Schuster, 1978), 35–39.
6. John 4:8–31 IV.
7. Peck, 312.
8. Madeleine L'Engle, *The Summer of the Great-Grandmother* (New York: Farrar, Straus and Giroux, 1974), 50.
9. I John 4:12 TEV.
10. Gerald Jampolsky, *Goodbye to Guilt* (New York: Bantam, 1985), 33.

MEDITATION

Our Desert

Our desert is any place where we confront God. It is not a change of scene, nor a place to run from our failures, nor a heroic adventure that does something for our ego.

Our desert experience may be tedium, weariness, disappointment, loneliness, personal emptiness, emotional confusion, the feeling that we have nothing to give, the conviction that we constantly fail God in prayer. You just have to keep on keeping on in prayer, and you are not aware of progress, because there seems to be nothing by which it could be measured. There are no paths in the desert except the ones you make by walking on them.

It is the place of truth, but also of tenderness—the place of loneliness, but also of God's closeness and care. The journey is precarious, but God is faithful, even though our own fidelity is shaky.

In the place of hunger and poverty of spirit we are fed by the word of God, as Jesus himself was in the desert. Part of our poverty may be that we are not even aware of longing for God, only aware of the suffocating burden of our own sinfulness, of the slum within.

But the desert is the place of confrontation not just with our sins, but with the power of God's redemption. You come to see it as the place where there can be springing water, manna to keep you going, the strength you never knew you had, the surprise of the quail that plops down at your feet, a tenderness that cares for you and a knowing of the Lord.

These things are not the promised land, but they are tokens of love and may be sacraments of glory. Your life, your prayer, can be the wilderness to which you must look steadfastly if you would see the glory of God.

—Maria Boulding[1]

Chapter 3

"Closure—A Sometimes Necessary Step"

Goals of this session:*

- To emphasize the value of closure as a responsible action in self-forgiveness
- To describe closure as a step toward forgiveness, not as forgiveness itself
- To stress the essential need for closure in some situations

Objectives:

- Participants will enact a conflict situation in which closure has taken place and discuss other alternatives.
- An activity to recount endings and beginnings will be shared.
- Several people will prepare a dialogue on closure and forgiveness and bring it to class.

---

*Note to teacher: Class activities will require advance preparation. Assignments will need to be given to participants the week before each class session.

The hope in every broken relationship is that reconciliation and restoration will occur. When that hope is dashed, creative ways are needed to redeem the alienation. One such way is closure.

While the restoration of a relationship demands forgiveness, closure may be part of the journey. It is a realistic way of recognizing an end in order to reach a point of beginning. It is not forgiveness, but without mutuality it may be a temporary shelter while one prepares for the hard journey to forgiveness. It is done by people who have an awareness of self-forgiveness. It is done carefully, so that it is never mistaken for the end of the journey. Closure establishes a new way of relating.

One contemporary form of closure is divorce. For centuries divorce was considered sinful and unacceptable by many Christians. The reality is that divorce happens. While it may be a heartbreaking choice both for those who choose the option and those who love them, it sometimes remains the only viable solution to some unhappy relationships. An article by John Shelby Spong illustrates one way that a couple established closure with self-forgiveness and created the possibility for further growth in each person and in those who love them. They met with their friends in their congregation to ritualize their decision to part:

The man and woman faced each other and spoke of their pain and failure, and of the seemingly inexorable nature of their separation; of loneliness and the need to learn new ways of relating; and of the sense of death, which both were experiencing. They asked each other for forgiveness, and pledged to be friends, to stand united in caring for their children and to be civil and responsible to each other. They thanked their friends for their willingness to share that moment of pain.

And it was painful for everyone there. All shared the excruciating pain of human brokenness, the irrevocable fracture in a relationship that had once brought joy and fulfillment. The divorced couple wept, and so did every member of the gathered group. Hearts cried out for an easy answer, for an embrace, for someone to say that this was a bad dream that would depart, leaving the past restored. But the service took place in real life, not in fantasy. The pain could not be removed; it had to be endured and transformed.[2]

Closure is a difficult decision. When persons invest in relationships, they do so expecting the commitment to last, whether that be marriage or friendship. Circumstances happen, however, in which commitments change. Closure sometimes makes possible self-acceptance. The experience of closure is not simply related to human interactions but may be understood in relationship to events or concepts.

For instance, when people move from a particular view of scripture to another, closure occurs. "I remember believing intensely that the words of scripture were literally the words of God," Jerry said. "Then, as I began to study and deal with the questions that plagued me, I came to a completely different place in my appreciation of scripture. I no longer look at those words as some direct quote that has come down a pipeline from God. They are, to me, the words of human beings expressing their understandings of the Divine." He continued by describing something of the grief he first experienced, then a sense of anger, and finally exhilaration. "I felt freed from a lot of burdening concepts when I closed the door to that point of view. For a long time I felt angry at the people who taught me about scripture, but now I understand that they shared what mattered to them. Closing the door to literalism was necessary for me."

CLOSURE MAY BE PAINFUL

Experiences such as Jerry's happen frequently, and people are able to move on to new understanding. For those who fail to recognize that they have made a decision to move to new terrain, however, there may be residual guilt and grief. This is particularly true if their new concepts are met with resistance by friends and family. Sometimes closure creates defensiveness, making the passage to forgiveness more difficult and less likely. Every change in life, even the most positive, is a grief process.

Closure places Jerry on new ground. If he fails to value his past and ridicules that which he once believed, then he will have difficulty relating to those who still stand in that place. Closure, understood as a shelter during an arduous journey, can move the forgiver forward.

More painful, however, are changes in relationships. Sometimes friends are no longer able to continue their association. A specific event may take place, or distance or time erode what was once creative communication. This may happen gradually enough that people simply move into other circles, but occasionally one of the friends becomes aware of the distance and the artificiality of the relationship. The distance becomes so great that neither person seems able to bridge the gap.

Such are the circumstances when marriages deteriorate. Often the couple could avoid closure if the distance were acknowledged and communication reestablished. When the gulf is too wide and the desire for reconciliation is not shared, divorce ends the marriage. For one of the parties the marriage may have ended some time before, but the divorce is necessary to close the relationship.

Closure seems contradictory to forgiveness. Since the definition of forgiveness includes the restoration of relationship, how can closure even be discussed?

It may be that ending a painful relationship makes possible the creation of a new one at some future time based on fresh understandings and experiences. The future may not offer such possibilities, but responsible closure is a healthy way to determine that the dignity of everyone involved is upheld.

When there is an unbridgeable distance between two people, both need to sense their own and the other's personal worth. Past models of forgiveness have sometimes suggested that one person give up everything to make reconciliation possible. This has been particularly true in traditional views of marriage. Generally this is possible only in a dependency relationship, not a mutual one. Yet, mature, freeing relationships—whether marriage or friendship—are mutual covenants between two people who love each other, not out of need but out of choice.

NEED FOR SELF-ESTEEM

Harry Stack Sullivan, an eminent American psychiatrist, asserts that "when the personal satisfaction or the security of another person becomes as significant to one as is one's own satisfaction or security, then the state of love exists." Sullivan commends such love as the only basis for sound marriages.[3]

This means that a sense of self-worth is vital in both partners in a marriage. When that worth is violated or distorted the couple may, of necessity, have to establish closure in order to be emotionally healthy. Such is not without heartrending pain and is merely a step *toward* forgiveness, not forgiveness itself.

DEALING WITH CLOSURE

Several years ago friends of ours determined that they could no longer remain married. They had spent years trying to work through irreconcilable divisions. They were now parting. Dick and I love them deeply and wanted to remain friends with both of them. We filled our cup of blessing and sat around our kitchen table the last Saturday evening they would be together as husband and wife. We passed the cup around the table and each of us sipped the juice and made a promise to the others to care for our friendship. We laughed, cried, and finally prayed together. The following week they separated, and each began a new life. We vowed to support them. I believe they are aware of our continued concern.

Their situation included anger, hostility, pain, grief, and loss. Other friends found themselves in awkward circumstances on several occasions, which added to the discomfort the divorced couple faced. But honesty about the struggle helped. Nurturing continues.

I have learned a great deal from the pain experienced with my friends. Closure is not as joyful for us as reconciliation would have been. But we cannot live their lives. Their decisions must be honored. Forgiveness is the work they do for themselves and with each other. Our responsibility in our friendship is to live in loving, creative, and open acceptance.

Since their decision was painful to us, our forgiveness may need to include our grief at their decision. We need to free ourselves of feelings of guilt that we failed them. They need to be supported in their decision, not criticized.

When others separate—sever their connections—I am not necessarily compelled to end my friendship with them. I do not take sides; I maintain an openness to them. Our friends' decision to end their marriage could have meant the cutting of our ties, but while we cannot prevent endings, we can use the closure to begin restorative beginnings.

Closure helps us learn that no human being can relate to everyone—that is the domain of God. In our humanity, we are broken and limited. Forgiveness reminds us of our human condition. By the grace of God, we are capable of healing and binding our brokenness, but alienation is real and is part of our daily experience.

Closure is a creative attitude when I confront people who do not love me. When I was growing up in the church community as a child and youth, I believed that the church family was like my own biological family who loved me, no matter what. Some of my church family, for their own reasons, could not love me. Like others, I have known people that I wanted to care for who did not respond to me. I cannot let the uncaring of others define me. I respect their decision and accept it. Their choice is not a reflection of my worth. They are moving on their journey, just as I must travel on mine.

ACCEPTING ENDINGS

What I can do when I am closed out of a relationship is to accept my own strength and gifts, love myself as God has commanded me to do, and move into wholesome relationships with those who do respond. When I do that, my pilgrimage is graced with endings and beginnings. Closure can become both. It helps me end an uncreative, destructive relationship;

it opens me to myself and the need to reestablish relationship with the Holy Spirit that dwells within.

Jesus acknowledged closure when he counseled, "Let the dead bury their dead."[4] There are times when our acceptance of death—both physical death and the end of relationships—is vital to our appreciation of life. Closure is not desired. It is often a result of unintended actions; yet despite its negative qualities it carries the clue to new possibilities. Closure acknowledges the breach. To pretend the separation does not exist, to act as though there were no break is to deny where we are on our journey. Where we are when we end a relationship becomes where we begin when we start anew on our sojourn.

CONFRONTING DEATH

Our travel may have stopped for a moment when we confront an ending. Death is a momentary end to a relationship. Sometimes people are unable to bear that loss, so they deny death when it happens. While they may act on the surface as though they accept their loss, at a deeper emotional level they refuse to acknowledge the reality.

A widowed friend of mine told me, "I learned the most important truth of my life following Don's death. I did not die from my grief. I continued to live. I am a survivor. I can take life as it comes and go forward. For some time, I refused to accept the reality that Don was dead. I had a little mental game I played where I convinced myself that he was away on one of his business trips, and pretty soon he would walk through the door. I didn't really start healing until I could accept the reality that he was not going to walk back through that door. Nothing I could do would make that happen. Now that I can accept his death, he seems more alive to me. I sense his presence more strongly."

Closure, in my friend's case, was not of her choosing. It happened to her. Her voyage of life was not as she planned it. However, if she wanted to maintain her mental health she had no choice but to accept her husband's death. All their beautiful memories were just that—memories. The poignant, bittersweet "once was" was over. But she learned to celebrate her past—good and bad—and to move on into the present.

A rape victim experiences a similar sense of helplessness at being subject to events over which she or he has no control. The person violated may never be able to confront the rapist. Studies indicate that rape victims have a higher than normal anxiety level throughout the remainder of their lives. The damage to self-esteem has traumatic effects. But these victims learn to use their experience creatively when they begin to recognize it as something they neither deserved nor asked for. Closure for this violation may take a lifetime, but persons can move from the "victim" self-image to that of "survivor." Rape counselors help them accept the past and then leave it behind. Such a decision is closure. Louise Garrison (see chapter 2) illustrates the wisdom of this course of action.

MOVING FROM GUILT AND SHAME

Closure is not repressing the past or denying it. It is full acceptance of what happened, a recognition of the limits of mutuality and reciprocity in the forgiving work, and a decision to act responsibly to oneself. Freedom from the guilt and shame, so often the lot of the violated, begins when the past is acknowledged and all self-recrimination ceases. When this happens, forgiveness is first experienced as self-acceptance. Forgiveness of the offender may take much longer. It may never be fully experienced. But that goal is possible only after the first step, closure.

Closure then may be an essential part of the process of forgiveness for many people. In some circumstances, it may be a place where some stay for a long time and then suddenly make huge strides on their journey.

The friend I met in the supermarket (chapter 1) needed to accept the end of her marriage. Closure might have enabled the forgiving process to begin. Instead, she rehearsed the painful events over and over. They became the only map to guide her life. She was bogged down in her own swamp of despair. The dead-end was her lack of self-acceptance. Her refusal to love herself kept her alienated from God just as surely as any treachery may have separated her from those she once loved. Once an action has taken place, those hurt by it must wrestle with its consequences. Self-forgiveness and closure can bring the freedom from guilt necessary for healing.

GENUINE FORGIVENESS

Closure may also prevent premature forgiveness. Christians may embrace forgiveness as an imperative, failing to realize that the process takes time.

Paul Tournier describes a patient who immediately forgave her husband's adultery. She was a devout Christian, and Tournier left for a trip amazed at the way her Christian faith made possible an immediate restoration of the relationship. Several weeks later, when he returned, he discovered she was suffering extreme depression and was physically ill.

Tournier began counseling with her and her husband. Genuine reconciliation took place after some long sessions over an extended period.[5] There is no timetable for forgiveness, and in some cases closure provides a necessary way station before the difficult pilgrimage begins.

For genuine forgiveness, I begin with the recognition that there has been an injury. If I discover that the work of forgiveness cannot be engaged in mutually, then I may have to accept closure as a means of rerouting my journey. I have to be willing to let go of the past and accept the burden that an ending has come. Closure may make possible future affinity. Meanwhile it creates an ending, or at least a detour. I have to take responsibility for my decision, however.

CLOSURE—A STOPPING PLACE

Christians remember the promises of God. When the disciples walked the road to Emmaus, they had closed the possibility of Jesus living. They had faced the real experience of the Crucifixion—of loss. They were surprised and brought into a new life when Christ met them there and shared with them.

Closure is a stopping place. If I leave myself open to the healing power of the Holy Spirit, I will find new strength to move from where I have stopped. When I decide to forgive someone who refuses to participate in the reconciliation, I will be ready for the pain and work required. I can remember this scriptural promise: "Do not cling to events of the past or dwell on what happened long ago. Watch for the new thing I am going to do. It is happening already—you can see it now!"[6] I am strengthened for my sojourn.

Activities

1. Tom and Ed are closest friends. A misunderstanding over a business deal causes some distance between them, and Ed chooses to close the friendship. Tom continues to try to sustain their relationship, only to be rebuffed by Ed. Tom discovers through a mutual friend that Ed blames him for the failed business venture. Ed refuses to communicate with Tom. What are Tom's options? Where is the gospel of reconciliation at work here? Will a third party serving as a caring mediator help? Have two people role play Tom and Ed. After a few minutes, invite someone to play the mediator. Afterward, discuss these questions. What are ways that people who have wounded each other may use to be brought together again? What is the role of closure? What possibilities are created if closure is refused? How are the families, friends, and church community affected by closure?

2. Following the discussion of Ed and Tom, have Someone recount the story of Louise Garrison (chapter 2). What possibilities for reconciliation are applicable to Louise? What is the responsibility of the church community to Tom and Ed? To Louise?

3. In groups of three or four, discuss the following rules for Endings and Beginnings.

Rules for Endings

Ask yourself what you learned from an ending experience and how you have grown because of it. Someday you may want to celebrate what the experience meant to you.

Allow yourself to grieve for what is past and what is over. Someday you may want to have a proper burial for what is now behind you.

Start envisioning your future without this part of you which is ending.

Rules for Beginnings

Begin not with the intention of never ending what you start but with the expectation to learn and grow.

Accept a new experience on its own terms. Do not try to repeat the past or duplicate what has been before.

Look at yourself every once in a while and try to get a picture of who you are and what you are becoming because of this new part of you.[7]

4. The week before this class session, ask one person to prepare a two-minute statement, "Closure is essential to self-forgiveness." Ask another to prepare a two-minute statement, "Closure is not forgiveness." The two may disagree with each other. Have these people present their statements in class. Encourage dialogue and openness. Ask the class to respond to specific issues in the statements.

5. In closing, sing together, "We Come Aware of Sin," HS 334.

NOTES

1. Maria Boulding, *The Coming of God* (Liturgical Press, 1983). Copyright © 1983 The Society for Promoting Christian Knowledge. Used by permission.
2. John Shelby Spong, "Can the Church Bless Divorce?" *Christian Century* (November 28, 1984), 1126. Copyright © 1984 Christian Century Foundation. Reprinted by permission from the Nov. 28, 1984, issue of *The Christian Century*.
3. Harry Stack Sullivan, *Concepts of Modern Psychiatry* (New York: W. W. Norton and Company, 1953), 42–43.
4. Matthew 8:22 IV.
5. Paul Tournier, *The Strong and the Weak*, trans. Edwin Hudson (Philadelphia: Westminster Press, 1963), 186–187.
6. Isaiah 43:18–19 TEV.
7. William Willimon, "Endings and Beginnings," *alive now!* (September/October 1979), 38–39. Copyright © 1979 *The Upper Room*; used by permission.

MEDITATION

Meditation for Healing Memories

The aim of our pilgrimage is to be transformed from within that we might perceive reality in a new way, experience the world in a new way, and live our lives in relationship to that world in ways that God's will might be done and God's kingdom come. For that to occur our journey has endings and beginnings.

Conversion, the change of mind or perception, the repentance to which a Christian is called, is a continuous and lifelong process. While conversions begin as everything in history does at some time, their processes are not completed until every aspect of the human personality is driven out into the light of God's mercy and renewed. Conversions proceed layer by layer, relationship by relationship, here a little, there a little—until the whole personality, intellect, feeling, and will have been recreated by God.

—John H. Westerhoff[1]

Chapter 4

Forgive and Re-member

Goals of this session:*
- To acknowledge the need to heal memories
- To consider the work of Matthew and Dennis Linn in "healing memories"
- To recognize the power of the past to continue to control our actions

Objectives:
- Participants will explore the damage of unhealed memories.
- Class members will discuss the use of the chart describing five stages of healing memories, and—working alone—critique an event from the past.
- Working in pairs, participants will engage in an exercise to heal a memory.
- Class members will discuss the encounter of U. S. President Ronald Reagan with Jewish writer Elie Wiesel.
- Examples of the power of healing memories as an act of re-membering (tying back together) will be shared.
- An activity of sharing forgiveness and bearing burdens will be offered.

---

*Note to teacher: Class activities will require advance preparation. Assignments will need to be given to participants the week before each class session.

Everyone carries deep hurts from the past. Some are repressed, others remembered with bitterness. Since closure is only a step toward forgiveness, the role of memory in forgiveness is essential. It is the painful memory that often keeps the process of forgiving from realization.

Almost any person can remember a time of hurt or neglect, a childhood embarrassment, humiliation by an adult, a friend who lied, a clerk who cheated. To confront these memories and allow them to speak to us may bring feelings of anger, hurt, disgust, betrayal—none of which are comfortable. But to confront the painful memories in the context of forgiveness is to discover unrealized strengths and to discover a new way to live.

POWER OF A PAINFUL PAST

"My father betrayed our family," Nancy told her counselor. "His infidelity affected all of us. I was very young, but I remember the pain my mother experienced, and my anger at Dad's absence." At the suggestion of the counselor, Nancy sat in front of an empty chair and began to speak as though it were to her father. Much of the pain of her childhood began to emerge. Her voice became higher—like that of a child. There were tears of anger and resentment. She spilled out all her hurt and frustration.

When the session was over, she began to weep, but her tears were different, and her face was relaxed. "My dad died a number of years ago," she said. "I always adored him, but I never grieved when he died. Now I can honestly grieve. I had to face the real pain in me before I could really love my father." This story came out of a "healing memories" session.

Nancy's grief over her father's death was now possible. Her denial of her past had allowed those events to control her life. Now she did not have to deny who her father was to love him. The acceptance was not forgiveness, but it was an essential step in the process. The memory needed to be healed for forgiveness to take place.

THE FOUNDATION OF MEMORIES

"We all have a need for painful memories to be healed, because to leave them unhealed is to allow them a powerful directing force in our lives," writes Doris Donnelly.[2] Thus, the activity of remembering is essential to forgiveness. Contrary to the popular saying that we "forgive and forget," we re-member (we put together again) and forgive, and forgive and remember. The cycle is essential.

Noted Jewish writer Elie Wiesel survived the Holocaust and uses that pivotal event as a creative force in his life. He believed that forgivers know "we cannot change events, but we can change meanings. That's our force."[3] To change meanings is to first deal with meanings from our past, to understand how they have affected us, and to use them creatively.

Frederick Buechner invites us to the "Room called Remember...to enter that still room within us all where the past lives on as part of the present, where the dead are alive again, where we are most alive ourselves to the long journeys of our lives with all their twistings and turnings and to where our journeys have brought us."[4]

Why is remembering so essential to forgiveness? Because it gives the forgiver a foundation on which to build a new life; because until the past is acknowledged and embraced, the future is held back. That which we refuse to claim in ourselves keeps whispering its mean little secrets to us. To move into the future as loving, liberated people requires an honesty about ourselves and a recognition of personal worth.

HEALING MEMORIES

Matthew and Dennis Linn have authored several books about healing memories. They believe that forgiveness is the key to physical and mental health. When a person buries a terrible memory in the subconscious, the Linns have discovered, memory controls. Once the memory is healed, so is the person.[5]

Since the work of Sigmund Freud, studies by psychiatrists have offered a wealth of supporting evidence for the release that accompanies the healing of memories. Often deep emotional or physiological problems develop from unhealed memories. Medical case studies are replete with examples of such crippling problems as paralysis, deafness, and blindness, which leave when the patient finally recalls the traumatic event which has been buried in the memory.

A student of the life and ministry of Jesus discovers the same principle in the record of Jesus' healings. Jesus integrates memory and forgiveness. Almost without fail, Jesus sends away the healed person with the promise, "Your sins are forgiven." Wholeness in body, mind, and spirit is integration. Such health demands dealing with the past.

A clear example of this is the story developed in the film, "The Stone Boy." A young teenager kills his older brother in a shooting accident. The boy is traumatized by the event and the movie unfolds the story of the resulting damage to the family. It also reveals the power of a caring grandparent who continues to accept the boy and walk with him through his pain. Only the boy can reconcile the event in himself, but the grandfather is there creating an environment in which healing can take place. Finally, when the boy is able to tell someone that he shot his brother, when he has tried to be reconciled with other members of the family, only then is he brought back to health. In order to be healed, he confronts the past and accepts the reality of the tragic event. Acceptance of reality is essential to the healing of grief.

"The Stone Boy" dramatizes the power of unhealed memory. Like the child in the story, each of us confronts painful memories that no one can take from us. We can refuse to allow ourselves to remember, however, and to do so is to fail to use our own lives redemptively. The power of the Holy Spirit and our own willingness to struggle can blend into acts of redemptive healing.

To grow, we have to forgive our past mistakes. We can do so only by honestly accepting them as such, then realizing that we are no longer the same. Our mistakes contribute to our growth when we accept them and forgive them. We can let them go. While it is usually uncomfortable to relive a mistake, it sometimes helps to do so and to be able to say, "I would not do that today. I have learned from that error, and I am stronger for the lesson it taught me." The past cannot be changed, but the way we look at it can be.

We are responsible for our attitude toward the past. We are responsible for our thoughts, and when we are able to change the way we think, we are also able to change our world.

That power to change thoughts is the exercise of healing memories. In the following chart, Matthew and Dennis Linn use the five stages of dying developed by Elisabeth Kubler-Ross as a model for healing memories:[6]

STAGES	IN DYING	IN HEALING A MEMORY
Denial	I don't ever admit I will die.	I don't admit I was ever hurt.
Anger	I blame others for letting death hurt and destroy me.	I blame others for hurting and destroying me.
Bargaining	I set up conditions to be fulfilled before I'm ready to die.	I set up conditions to be fulfilled before I'm ready to forgive.
Depression	I blame myself for letting death destroy me.	I blame myself for letting hurt destroy me.
Acceptance	I look forward to dying.	I look forward to growth from hurt.

The Linns believe that memories can be healed in such a way that the person who has been wounded will be able not only to say, "I forgive" to those responsible for the pain, but will also experience gratitude for the growth that forgiveness made possible. This is a monumental shift for people who have experienced violence or abuse and may take a lifetime to achieve. However, when a person arrives at that stage of forgiveness, then certainly the meaning of the original event has been transformed.

The Linns consider memories "like an iceberg" and "unconditional love is like the blazing sun." Their analogy describes the iceberg melting as it is exposed to the heat of the sun. "Doing healing of memories every day, either alone or with others, I find that deeper and deeper parts of the submerged unconscious get exposed to the Lord's warmth and tenderness."[7] They believe that healing of memories is a continual, daily process which is part of the meditation and prayer life of the Christian. Most Christian writers agree, acknowledging that forgiving memories is essential to a healthy relationship and permits the flow of love to others.

USING THE PAST CREATIVELY

Forgiveness, then, is more than just accepting the past. It is actively using previous pain and joy to arrive at a new way station. It is a conscious act in which we are able to develop self-love as well as compassion for others. The act of healing memories is to engage in an exercise in which we deliberately confront something which has hurt us deeply. The choice to do this may be difficult. It is more than just accepting that something happened, or that what happened was painful. It is a choice to recognize that someone has hurt us and to actively engage in an exercise to free that person from the offense. In so doing, we become free ourselves.

Acceptance of the past is essential to forgiveness, but it is not forgiveness itself. It is much like a part in a machine. The machine may not work without the part, but the part cannot function as the machine. Forgiveness is more complex than acceptance. I begin to heal a memory by accepting that something terrible happened to me. This is but a step in the process; more is required to heal the memory.

Since one cannot change the past, healing the memory is an essential route on the journey toward forgiveness. One cannot look back at the past and demand it be just if acts of injustice were done. But to heal the memory of that event requires a commitment to justice by those who hold the memory.

JUSTICE IS VITAL

In a controversial decision, U.S. President Ronald Reagan went to Bitberg cemetery in Germany in 1985. He believed this to be an act of reconciliation. He was unaware that a number of SS soldiers were buried there when he made the decision, but even upon learning that, he continued to affirm the rightness of his course of action. The Jewish community in the United States pleaded with him to change his itinerary. Elie Wiesel, at a ceremony where he received a medal for his outstanding humanitarian efforts, confronted the president with the feelings of Jews about the decision to go to Bitberg. For Wiesel, the meaning of the Holocaust was demeaned by the president's decision. A commitment to justice, for Wiesel, was to acknowledge the horror of the events of the Nazi regime and to keep that horror before people so that it can never happen again—to hold justice up as a model.

The president's decision continues to elicit controversy, but certainly Wiesel's premise regarding justice is essential to forgiveness. David Augsburger, in defining "false forgiveness," reminds us that "when forgiveness foregoes repentance, and forgets the enduring unresolved issues of justice, don't rush to it, don't be taken in by it."[8]

One way, then, that memories are healed is through acts of justice. The mother whose son was killed by a drunken driver commits herself to acts of justice when she organizes a movement against drunken driving. The victim of the nuclear holocaust in Hiroshima who works for peace and disarmament is healthier emotionally, suggests Dr. Robert Jay Lifton who has worked with survivors, than those who do not.[9] Justice is redemptive, and the memories that destroy are those unconfronted and kept alive by bitterness, malice, and unforgiveness. These are the memories that are often the root of illnesses such as ulcers, hypertension, and other stress-related diseases.

In her book *Ordinary People,* Judith Guest describes how the tragic drowning of one of the sons leads to the deterioration of the family. The surviving son, Conrad, attempts suicide. An encounter with his psychiatrist depicts the beginning of Conrad's healing. Weary with the constant memory of the death of his brother, Conrad suffers enormous guilt that he, Conrad, survived. Finally, he confronts the memory and walks into its pain. He begins to understand that self-punishment doesn't banish his guilt. The wise psychiatrist reminds him that "the guilt doesn't make the memory go away. And it doesn't earn you any forgiveness. . . . So what's the point of it then?"[10]

If I hold to an unforgiven memory, I punish myself—either with guilt or bitterness. This only keeps me locked into the agony of that event. It doesn't help me deal with my own responsibility to myself. It doesn't make the pain go away, and it certainly doesn't help me experience the freedom I yearn for. It makes sense to deal with the memory, to forgive it, and to move into the present and future unencumbered.

In a song of social justice, Bernice Johnson Reagon brings another dimension to the meaning of healing

memories: "The sounds of struggle you hear...
are...nothing but the echoes of the past."[11] This is
probably the most dangerous and critical aspect of
unhealed memories. The action is often repeated.

When we have wronged another and have refused
to face our actions we are almost doomed to repeat
that pattern of behavior. Addictive personalities bear
this out when despite their repeated desire to repent
and change, they continue to abuse themselves and
those who love them. Repeated offenders of crimes
against persons often express a desire to change but
continue their destructive actions. "The echoes of
the past" may be deeds we want to forget, both in our
personal life and on a national scale, but our behavior is not likely to change until we heal the
memory of what we have done or of what has been
done to us.

STOP THE RERUNS OF PAIN

The Linns suggest that, for some people, the healing of memories is a long-time process which involves much effort and willingness to suffer through
the pain of the past, while for others, it seems to occur overnight. But one measurement of healing is
when we can be grateful for the lessons learned from
the past event. They say the final stage of healing a
memory, like the final stage of dying, is acceptance.
"We are not loved unless we love Christ more and he
loves more through us. We are in the final stage, acceptance, only if we have a grateful heart given to
Christ for his love to touch those we touch."[12]

Lewis Smedes describes unhealed memories as re-
plays of old hurts: "a videotape within your soul that
plays unending reruns of your old rendezvous with
pain....You become addicted to your remembrance
of pain past." The pain of the memory does not leave

until we decide to risk the creative sojourn of forgiveness. "The only way to heal the pain that will not heal itself is to forgive the person who hurt you. Forgiving stops the reruns of pain. Forgiving heals your memory as you change your memory's vision," Smedes says.[13] It is in a person's own self-interest to forgive, to heal a hurtful memory, because to fail to do so is to choose to stay in bondage.

When Santayana wrote, "Those who refuse to remember the past are doomed to repeat it,"[14] he was offering good advice about forgiveness, too. We "remember" the history of hurt we have refused to remember lest we repeat that which we despise. The battered child (without forgiven memories) becomes a batterer. The alcoholic's child (without forgiven memories) becomes an alcoholic. The cycle is broken by forgiveness. A new reality is created by redemptive remembering. The painful "echoes of the past" become impetus for justice and reconciliation.

Activities

1. Meet with another person and remember an uncomfortable event from childhood. Perhaps a teacher was unkind, another child bullied you, or a parent was unjust. Take about three to five minutes to recall the event. On a sheet of paper, write the names of those involved, including your own name. Write words that depict feelings such as anger, sadness, frustration, loneliness. Ask your partner to acknowledge those feelings. "You feel sad," "You are angry," or whatever response will affirm your feelings. Now tell the event the way you would like for it to have happened. What are your feelings now? What is the difference when you deal with the memory as it happened and as you wish it had happened? Then, in silence, remember. Pull together in your mind the faces of all the people who were involved. Now, imagine yourself as each of those people. Can you enter into their feelings? What might have been going on in each of their lives? How do you feel now? If there is a difference when you remember, describe it. If not, ask your partner to offer a prayer for the healing of the memory. See yourself walking into a warm, sunny place where your memory is brought as a large piece of ice. As your partner prays for you and your release from the past, see the sun melting the ice. Let the people in the memory be freed from their past actions. As your partner prays, see if you can pray for those people who have wounded you.

2. Use the chart from the Linns' book, *Healing Life's Hurts*. Each member of the class may re-

member something someone has done to cause pain which needs to be forgiven. Ask the question, Where on the chart are you? In which stage are you in the forgiving process?

3. Using the same chart, remember something for which you wish to be forgiven. Where do you think you are in asking for forgiveness?

4. Ask two members of the class to participate in a debate, each speaking three minutes. One should take the position of President Reagan that the trip to the Bitberg cemetery is an essential act of forgiveness. The other should take the position of Elie Wiesel that to go there is to demean the past and trivialize the Holocaust. Ask the class to consider what acts of justice can be done to heal the memory of the Nazi slaughter of six million Jews.

5. Discuss the example from the "The Stone Boy." What acts of forgiveness can you imagine the young boy experienced (for those who may not have seen the movie) in order to reach a point of acceptance? Why was it essential that he remember before he could grieve?

6. Ask the class to respond to the statement by the psychiatrist in *Ordinary People*. How does guilt impede the forgiveness of memories? Discuss.

7. Sing together "Help Us Accept Each Other," *HS* 171.

NOTES

1. John H. Westerhoff, *The Spiritual Life: Learning East and West* (Winston Press [Seabury], 1982). Used by permission of Harper and Row, Publishers, Inc.
2. Doris Donnelly, *Learning to Forgive* (New York: Macmillan Publishing Compny, 1979), 37.
3. Harry James Cargas, *In Conversation with Elie Wiesel* (New York: Paulist Press, 1976), 104–105.
4. Frederick Buechner, *A Room Called Remember, Uncollected Pieces* (San Francisco: Harper and Row, 1984), 6.
5. Dennis Linn and Matthew Linn, *Healing Life's Hurts* (New York: Paulist Press, 1978), Chapter 4.
6. Ibid., 11. Used by permission of Paulist Press.
7. Ibid., 216.
8. Augsburger, 73.
9. Robert Jay Lifton discusses confrontation of the past and the need to address guilt in all of his works. Of particular significance to this chapter are *Death in Life: Survivors of Hiroshima* (New York: Simon and Schuster, 1976) and *The Broken Connection* (New York: Simon and Schuster, 1979).
10. Judith Guest, *Ordinary People* (New York: Ballantine Books, 1976), 210.
11. Bernice Johnson Reagon, "Echo," *Good News*, Sweet Honey in the Rock, Soundtrack Wilmington 10 U.S.A. Songtalk Publishing Company, 1979.
12. Linn, 176.
13. Lewis Smedes, *Forgive and Forget* (San Francisco: Harper and Row, 1984), 133.
14. George Santayana, revised by the author in collaboration with Daniel Cory, "Reason in Common Sense," *Life of Reason*, Vol. 1 (New York: Charles Scribner's Sons, 1953), 82.

MEDITATION

When the Goers Are Gone

Map said the road went through, but grass and growth argued it didn't; and the beaver dam mucked out the last bones of its skeleton. What makes a path able to say I am except for people constantly astride it trudging, marching, riding, foot and wheel tattooing the familiar pattern loud? The going and the goers make the road real.

—*Thomas John Carlisle*[1]

Chapter 5

Points of Departure

Goals of this session:*

- To see each of Jean Lambert's seven aspects of forgiving as a point of departure in the journey of forgiveness
- To explore each of the points as it relates to human experience
- To engage in dialogue about each point
- To continue to explore images of forgiveness as a journey

Objectives:

- Participants will describe their own journey of forgiveness using Jean Lambert's seven points of forgiving.
- Class members will illustrate the points, using their own experiences with forgiving.
- Exercises in mutuality will be conducted.

---

*Note to teacher: Class activities will require advance preparation. Assignments will need to be given to participants the week before each class session.

When a person begins a journey, there is usually a planned arrival point. Sometimes, however, in the course of the journey a new place is discovered or the traveler may stop longer than planned. When a trip is scheduled by the airlines, it may involve a stopover at some place along the way.

When we travel, we often think only of the place of departure and the place of arrival. However, on our journey we can discover some extraordinary terrain if we are open to discovery.

This is true for the journey of forgiveness, also. Because there are no formulas to offer the forgiver, we are wise to stay open to points of departure. When we decide to participate in the work of forgiveness, we have begun the journey.

Jean Lambert, in her book *The Human Action of Forgiving,* outlines seven characteristics in nearly every forgiving relationship. People who forgive discover that

1. Forgiving is a real possibility.
2. Forgiving pertains to personal relationships.
3. Forgiving becomes relevant when a break has taken place.
4. Forgiving implies judgment against the interpersonal wrong done or the injury.
5. Forgiving includes a decision about trust, namely to trust the original relationship rather than the break or the event that occasioned it.
6. Forgiving includes observable behavior that embodies or "acts out" judgment, mutual trust, and openness to the future.
7. Forgiving results in a restored relationship that is historical, free, and mutual.[2]

The real possibility of forgiveness depends on the conviction of people engaged in an act of mutual healing. If only one person is certain that forgiveness is possible, there is little chance that the relationship will be restored. In acts of closure, this is evident. One person cannot create a relationship. It takes two people to rebuild after damage has been done.

Corrie ten Boom describes this principle in *The Hiding Place*. She was the speaker in a church in Munich after World War II and recognized one of the people that evening as a former SS guard from the processing center where she, her sister, and other women prisoners had been held captive during the war. She remembered the horrible, humiliating treatment by the guards. During that evening she had testified of the forgiveness of sin through the gift of Christ Jesus. Only her conviction that forgiveness was a possibility permitted the following:

His hand was thrust out to shake mine. And I, who had preached so often to the people in Bloemendaal the need to forgive, kept my hand at my side.... Even as the angry, vengeful thoughts boiled through me, I saw the sin of them. Jesus Christ had died for this man; was I going to ask for more? Lord Jesus, I prayed, forgive me, and help me to forgive him.

I tried to smile. I struggled to raise my hand. I could not. I felt nothing, not the slightest spark of warmth or charity. And so again, I breathed a silent prayer. Jesus, I cannot forgive him. Give me Your forgiveness.

As I took his hand, a most incredible thing happened. From my shoulder along my arm and through my hand a current seemed to pass from me to him, while into my heart sprang a love for this stranger that almost overwhelmed me.[3]

She continues her testimony with the affirmation that the gift of God's forgiveness makes possible such an experience. God not only commands us to love our enemies, but gives us the love itself. Such belief creates the possibilities of forgiveness.

Corrie ten Boom and the guard were freed by her conviction that forgiveness and freedom are possible. Yet, she had to arrive at this place through her own decisions. No one had the right to demand her forgiveness.

MOVING BEYOND STEREOTYPES

This event, however, also emphasizes the second step of forgiving. The encounter between the Dutch woman and her German guard was a personal one. They were no longer prisoner and guard once the process of forgiving had begun. They were two human beings now, capable of a new relationship guaranteed in the forgiving love of God but essentially real only when it was experienced in their interaction.

Another way to understand this step is to recognize the damage done by categories, stereotypes, and labels. These attitudes keep human beings distanced. Forgiving sets in motion forces which span that distance.

When Sam retired from the university, he felt he was treated unfairly. Many of the progressive projects he had begun which meant new opportunities for minority students were shelved the year after he left. He felt betrayed by an administration that had, he felt, been dishonest in dealing with him. For months following retirement, he suffered hypertension, headaches, and even some heart disorders. His health was deteriorating when he began to realize that he had created an enemy out of the administrative structures at the college. His adversary wore no particular face, although the other vice-president with whom he had had the most disagreements often came up in his criticism of the university.

When his doctor began to probe into Sam's personal situation in an effort to determine the source of his physiological problems, she discovered that Sam had refused to deal with the problem of personal relationships with his former workers. She suggested that rather than using tranquilizers, Sam might be healthier if he took one or two of the administrators to lunch and shared his frustration, hurt, and anger.

On her recommendation, he did. While Sam was no longer a part of the decision-making body, he was able to establish a new relationship with his former co-workers. Some of them did not understand his need to meet with them; some were even critical of his attitudes. But Sam was helped by the encounter. He was able to explain his concerns without being defensive. He was also able to talk about his disappointments without being critical.

The meeting and Sam's willingness to be open and vulnerable set in motion new opportunities for communication. He felt enormous release from tension. His blood pressure problems were resolved. He slept better. Now he could talk freely about his disappointments without needing to blame anyone. He could also begin to build honest, creative relationships with people whose ideas were quite different from his own.

Sam's journey began in his willingness to claim his responsibility to the relationships and to care enough to try to bridge the gap. Because of the break, forgiving was essential.

Forgiving is particularly relevant in family relationships when a break has taken place. The break may be the simple act of rebellion (often necessary to growth in adolescence). Or it may be a wounding experience in a marriage—unkind criticisms, infidelity, or failure to respond to needs. Whatever created the chasm, forgiving is relevant when the break is recognized.

A traditional Christian response has been to say, "I'm sorry," and to expect these words to heal the breach. But people who work in human relationships say that mutual relationships call for mutual responsibility.

Thus, the journey of forgiveness calls for a recognition of the interpersonal wrong done or the injury. To accept that a wrong has been done is an act of judgment. To judge, according to Webster's dictionary, is to "hear and determine." Thus, while judgment implies criticism and is sometimes thought of primarily as condemnation, its critical nature can be redemptive. To view judgment in a negative way can be a distortion of its essential quality. Judgment is more than censure; it is "to form an authoritative opinion" about an action.

Therefore, decisions must be made in forgiving. These critical opinions require that both parties understand the damage done and mutually decide to acknowledge the hurt. This is more than recognizing the destructive action and finding "a guilty party." Judgment here implies justice. It calls for confrontation. It requires honesty. Those who participate in forgiveness must acknowledge the hurt. Such a judgment is difficult for both the one who seeks forgiveness and the one who must extend it.

Often at this point, there is a temptation to use the categories of offender and offended. Living free of such labels moves one on the journey. The person must be forgiven, but a judgment must be made about the action. Such an open stance is difficult for some. "Certainly I can forgive *you*, but I'll never forgive what you *did*," is to say, "I am not yet ready to participate in forgiveness."

If, however, a person can arrive at the place where judgment is made about the act, rather than against the person, then the journey toward trust has begun. It is essential to trust the original relationship rather than the break or the event that occasioned it.

TRUST THE ORIGINAL RELATIONSHIP

The journey may get rugged here. When someone has been betrayed, humiliated, or injured, pain of the event seems stronger than the original relationship. The break that occasioned the need for forgiveness often becomes the stopping place. My friend in the supermarket (see chapter one) had not even arrived here. She had stopped at the point of alienation and had stayed there for fifteen years, becoming more entrenched each passing day.

To trust the original relationship requires using the powerful tool, memory, and recalling the times of caring that initially undergirded the relationship prior to the alienation.

Such was Ethel's experience. Her daughter, Susan, was planning her wedding and wanted both her parents to attend, but Ethel and Tom had been divorced for some time. Tom married shortly after the divorce, and Ethel felt a great deal of hostility toward Sally, his second wife. Ethel wanted nothing to do with either Tom or Sally. Her love for Susan was strong, though, and she began preparations for her daughter's celebration. One evening, just prior to the wedding, Tom and Sally had to stop by Ethel's home to bring Susan a package. Just as they arrived, Ethel had found a box of photographs from a family vacation taken when Susan was young. Despite the initial awkwardness of the meeting with Tom and Sally, as she began recalling with Tom some of the happy memories of their early life, she was able to rejoice in the past in a way she had not done for years.

Later that evening, when she was alone, Ethel realized that while she and Tom would probably never again be close friends, there were bridges to be built both for her own mental health and for the happiness of their children. She determined to trust the feelings of regard and respect that she and Tom once held for each other. This freed her to move into a comfortable relationship with him and with Sally. Without this forgiveness Ethel would have continued to live in blame and judgment about Tom and Sally; this would have kept her from growing and finding new joy in life.

LIVING IN CHANGE

Life is change. Sometimes the changes seem to "happen to us." However, we are each responsible for the way we use the changes that happen. When they take place, we can use the events for growth or refuse to move beyond the point of departure. Fixed in distrust, we create our own misery.

For those who desire a mutual relationship and for whom there has been an event which occasioned a break, this particular step offers rich possibilities. Bernard Loomer, in a monograph, "Two Kinds of Power," illustrates how brokenness can open us to greater depths of experience:

An infidelity in marriage can lead to a deeper level of maturity in the relationship than perhaps was possible before. In the biblical parable of the prodigal son the deeply resentful older brother is given the possibility of a growth in stature in the face of the father's joyous welcoming of the repentant younger brother. The naughtiness of young children can call out depths within the parents which were not exemplified previously. The presence of evil does not lead inevitably to a greater good. Obviously. But the actualization of greater good seems to be grounded on brokenness in some degree.[4]

In the midst of evil, the possibility for goodness resides. In the midst of terrible alienation, forgiveness makes reconciliation possible.

"To be where I am now, I would go through all the pain I've known with my parents," Elaine said. "I am much closer to them than I ever dreamed possible." Forgiveness for Elaine was a way of using what had happened during the years of rebellion as a place to begin anew.

She began realizing her parents' fears and her own role in the hostility she felt at home. Accepting responsibility and reaching out to her mother and father, she discovered two enjoyable adults she wanted to know better. The difficult years behind had taught all three people how important they were to each other.

Such reconciliation as Elaine and her parents enjoyed is not guaranteed. People sometimes choose to remain distanced from each other. The bridges, however, are more likely to occur with forgiveness. Without it, little changes.

FORGIVENESS REQUIRES RELATIONSHIP

Elaine's experience illustrates Lambert's sixth principle: forgiving includes observable behavior that embodies or "acts out" judgment, mutual trust, and openness to the future. If Elaine's efforts at reconciliation had been rejected, then her future with her parents would be questionable. Her judgment of herself was essential. So was her willingness to trust her parents after years of distrust. Their mutual response—a willingness to accept their responsibility in the separation, and their willingness to trust Elaine—embodied forgiving.

Unless forgiving is lived out in a relationship, nothing changes. Theories of forgiveness, reading scriptures about forgiveness, even prayers for forgiveness finally have to be enacted between the separated people.

"It was not enough that Jennifer promise me that she would not lie to me again," her mother said. "I had to see that she was honest." Broken trust is difficult to restore. Observable behavior helps heal past betrayals. Yet the person who has first broken the trust must also be able to trust the one who has been betrayed. Lying is often a manifestation of deeper divisions between people. Jennifer had to learn to trust her mother's ability to trust her. The paradox here is that trust becomes both gift and work. When an environment of distrust exists, usually both parties contribute to it. People who can trust themselves are most likely to be trustworthy.

Jennifer's mother began to trust her daughter after they had spent some time discussing the reasons for previous distrust. Repentance was needed by both parties. Jennifer was able to demonstrate her honesty when she knew that her mother expected honesty and was willing to confront her when there were reasons to question it. Confrontation in the spirit of caring and trust carries a different message than confrontation based on suspicion.

REPENTANCE—AN ESSENTIAL STEP

Repentance is an essential step in true forgiveness. It usually follows a willingness to accept responsibility for one's past. Honesty is an integral part of repentance.

Scriptural accounts of forgiving events demonstrate this. When Jesus went to Zaccheus the tax collector, Zaccheus recognized what he had done to the members of his society and was deeply repentant. It was, however, when he acted justly that the forgiveness was realized.

The realization of forgiveness results "in a restored relationship that is historical, free, and mutual." Both Zaccheus and the people participated in the restoration of his place in the community.

Charles Dickens captures these principles in his immortal *Christmas Carol* with the account of the restoration of Ebenezer Scrooge to his community. Scrooge faced death itself and recognized what his tightfisted bondage was doing to him and to those around him. But when he did finally accept responsibility for his actions his acts of restoration liberated him from his selfish, lonely life of imprisonment to money.

Persons whose journey is forgiving share something of the joy Scrooge knew Christmas morning when he realized that he was alive and had another chance. Forgiveness gives us another chance—a new day.

That new day awaits those who move toward forgiving. Jean Lambert's map is one guide; there are many others. More significant than the route we choose for the journey is the commitment to begin. Whenever we open ourselves to forgiveness, to its creative, restoring power, we may hear in our hearts, the echo of Jesus' words to Zaccheus, "This day is salvation come."⁵

St. Francis of Assisi's prayer, "Make me an instrument of Thy peace," offers us the promise inherent in that salvation: "It is in pardoning that we are pardoned." Such redemptive power is healing and hope.

Activities

1. Give each member of the class a letter-size sheet of paper. Assign a map-drawing project. Using the seven steps suggested by Jean Lambert (page 86), draw a route to forgiveness. As the person creates the map, suggest that the easiest places be designated; those that seem more difficult might be described as mountains to climb or rivers to cross. Then ask the class to organize in pairs and share their maps. The following illustrates a possible map.

7. Forgiving results in a restored relationship that is historical, free, and mutual.

6. Forgiving includes observable behavior that embodies or "acts out" judgment, mutual trust, and openness to the future.

4. Forgiving implies judgment against the interpersonal wrong done or the injury.

5. Forgiving includes a decision about trust, namely to trust the original relationship rather than the break or the event that occasioned it.

3. Forgiving becomes relevant when a break has taken place.

2. Forgiving pertains to personal relationships.

1. Forgiving is a real possibility.

2. Following the map-drawing exercise, suggest that each pair meet with two other pairs, making six members in each group. Allow about twenty minutes for each group to come up with at least one illustration for each of the seven principles. If these are from personal experiences, they may be shared freely if the participants so desire. If they are from other people's experiences, ask class members to conceal identities of the persons about whom they speak in respect for privacy. This may be done by changing the location of the event, or the age or sex of the individual.

The seven principles can be addressed with some questions like these:

a. Forgiving is a real possibility. (Can a member of the group cite an incident in which he or she was convinced that reconciliation was possible? What led to that conviction?)

b. Forgiving pertains to personal relationships. (Why is this an important step on the journey? When have you known that forgiving was needed?)

c. Forgiving becomes relevant when a break has taken place. (At what point did you or someone you know become aware that there was a break in the relationship? Was your first concern forgiveness? If not, why? When did forgiveness seem timely?)

d. Forgiving implies judgment against the interpersonal wrong done or the injury. (How can one judge an action and not the person who committed that deed? How is that judgment enacted so that forgiving can occur? Why is this a vital step in the journey? Cite an incident in which you were able to judge something that happened to you as an injury and still create the climate for forgiveness.)

e. Forgiving includes a decision about trust—namely to trust the original relationship rather than the break or the event that occasioned it. (What kinds of discipline are necessary in this step? How does one re-create trust when it has been broken? Is this a step you would always be able to take? Describe a situation that might make restored trust difficult or impossible.)

f. Forgiving includes observable behavior that embodies or "acts out" judgment, mutual trust, and openness to the future. (Why is this essential? What is difficult about mutual trust? What role does judgment play in this?)

g. Forgiving results in a restored relationship that is historical, free, and mutual. (Can people let the past go? How? What does it mean to have a restored relationship that is historical? free? mutual?)

3. The following exercises may not be possible for everyone in the class because of physical disabilities or other reasons. If so, ask two or three pairs of people to demonstrate for the entire class. These exercises are designed to demonstrate mutual vulnerability. Ask each person to choose a partner evenly matched in size. When they are ready, have them stand, one person facing the other's back. Have the person in back link his or her arms around the neck of the partner and collapse, allowing the weight of the body to "drag." The other partner attempts to move, dragging the weight. This exercise demonstrates how unequal power in relationships

creates a burden. It also illustrates the power of unforgiven events which continue to drag a non-forgiver down and prevent the realization of mutuality.

4. Now, using the same partners try the following exercise in mutual support. The partners should stand facing each other about three feet apart. Have them stretch their arms forward at a forty-five degree angle from the floor. Now ask them to press their palms against those of their partners who are at the same position. Keeping hands together, step backwards simultaneously. The weight of both bodies will begin to exert pressure on the palms of the partners as they move farther apart. Move as far apart as possible. If possible, hold this position for two or three minutes. The partners should try to remain silent. If possible, look into each other's eyes. Try to keep supporting each other mutually.

5. Following the exercise, ask some of these questions:
Were you aware of mutual dependency?
Were you aware of your vulnerability to your partner? (If the exercise is done correctly, the balance of the partners is all that keeps them from falling forward.)
Did you feel greater trust for your partner after the activity?

6. Conclude the class by singing, "The Love of God," HS 107.

NOTES

1. Thomas John Carlisle, *alive now!* (March/April 1984), 35. Used by permission of the author.
2. Jean Lambert, *The Human Action of Forgiving: a Critical Application of the Metaphysics of Alfred North Whitehead* (Lanham, Maryland: University Press of America, Inc., 1985), Chapter 4, Section B2. Reprinted by permission of the publisher.
3. Corrie ten Boom, *The Hiding Place* (Old Tappan, New Jersey: Fleming H. Revell, Spire Books, 1971), 238. Used by permission of Chosen Books Inc. *The Hiding Place* by Corrie ten Boom with John and Elizabeth Sherrill. Published by Chosen Books Inc., Chappaqua, N.Y.
4. Bernard Loomer, "Two Kinds of Power," *Criterion* (Winter 1976): 27. Used by permission.
5. Luke 19:1–10 IV.

MEDITATION

At the time when the slaves in America were without any excuse for hope and they could see nothing before them but the long interminable cotton rows and the fierce sun and the lash of the overseer, what did they do? They declared that God was not through. They said, "We cannot be prisoners of this event. We must not scale down the horizon of our hopes and our dreams and our years to the level of the event of our lives...."

So long as you recognize that no event of your life, whatever its character, can imprison you, you will not scale down your aspirations to the level of the facts in your present situation. You will let what rides on the horizon constantly inform the event with which you are wrestling, until at last the event itself begins to open up, to yield, to break down, to disintegrate, under the relentless pressure of some force which transcends the event and tutors and informs it. That is what the Resurrection is all about.

—Howard Thurman[1]

Chapter 6

A Giant Step—Forgiveness as Global Politics

Goals of this session:*

- To understand forgiveness as a practical work in the world community
- To recognize the interdependence of forgiveness, power, justice, and love
- To image forgiveness as possibility for world politics

Objectives:

- Participants will "role-play" a forgiver and the recipient of forgiveness.
- Forgiveness as a possible way to world peace will be discussed.
- Forgiveness as self-interest will be explored.
- Class members will share with each other stories of forgiveness that have altered a political arena.

---

*Note to teacher: Class activities will require advance preparation. Assignments will need to be given to participants the week before each class session.

The cover story for *Time* magazine, January 9, 1984, chronicled a religious event. In the words of the reporter, "In a bare, white-walled cell in Rome's Rebibbia prison, John Paul tenderly held the hand that had held the gun that was meant to kill him. For 21 minutes, the Pope sat with his would-be assassin, Mehmet Ali Agca."

The Pope's act of forgiveness was international news. In a magazine that weekly publishes news of violence, war, and despair, this act was the featured event. It was treated as the symbol of "the Christian message." The writer suggested that "the scene may be important because it suggests that human beings can respond to inhuman acts by being sane and civilized and forbearing."

The article detailed the difficulty translating the Pope's action toward Agca as public policy. It did, however, emphasize forgiveness as "a profound transaction...the working model of the human relationship with God." Forgiveness, the authors concluded, "makes possible both spiritual change and social change."[2]

Since that time, Agca has been engaged in a trial. The Pope's act did not make him immune from the systems of justice. There were many international implications of the event which are so complex that it may be impossible to use the event in the Rebibbia jail cell as any kind of model.

There is something profound, though, in the symbol. Throughout the world, terrorism is on the increase. Hostility seems an acceptable way to deal with the enemy, and the enemy becomes any one or any nation with an ideology other than one's own.

Where in such an incomprehensible scenario does the act of forgiveness make sense?

It may very well be that the truth of forgiveness is its irrationality, its sheer folly in a world where enemies are logical, and fear is sound.

Forgiveness may be the quantum leap for world politics. A quantum leap, no matter how small, always makes a sharp break with the past. In scientific terms it is the discontinuous jump of an electron from one orbit to another, with the particle mysteriously leaving no trace of its path. However, it is also the link between two entirely separate locations, events, or ideas—that magical moment when the previously unexplainable is suddenly clear and a radical new theory is born.

One person may be able to take such a leap, leaving the past behind—but how can nations or interest groups move on that journey?

Perhaps no other quality is so needed in the journey toward world peace. There are countless occasions when human beings are violated by systems and structures over which they have little control. Laws designed to protect some people violate the rights of others. Benefits for some are enormous burdens for others. Technology, intended to enrich, seems to control and sometimes destroy the quality of life. Issues beyond understanding end up being critical to our lives.

FORGIVENESS AS SELF-INTEREST

Perhaps it would be useful to think of forgiveness as other than altruistic. Maybe it should be considered central to individual survival. It may be the most important action we make for ourselves. There may be no other position that will save the human race. Yet forgiveness is rarely seen as a quality of self-interest.

Dostoevsky, the great Russian novelist, wrote a parable which illustrates forgiveness as self-interest:

It's like this. Once upon a time there was a peasant woman, and a very wicked woman she was. And she died and did not leave a single good deed behind. The devils caught her and plunged her into a lake of fire. So her guardian angel stood and wondered what good deed of hers he could remember to tell God; "She once pulled up an onion in her garden," said he, "and gave it to a beggar woman." And God answered: "You take that onion then, hold it out to her in the lake, and let her take hold and be pulled out. And if you can pull her out of the lake, let her come to Paradise, but if the onion breaks, then the woman must stay where she is." The angel ran to the woman and held out the onion to her; "Come," said he, "catch hold and I'll pull you out." And he began cautiously pulling her out. He had just pulled her right out, when the other sinners in the lake, seeing how she was being drawn out, began catching hold of her so as to be pulled out with her. But she was a very wicked woman and she began kicking them. "I'm to be pulled out, not you. It's my onion, not yours." As soon as she said that, the onion broke. And the woman fell into the lake and she is burning there to this day. So the angel wept and went away.[3]

This parable illustrates the hell of privatism, of self-preservation. The woman in the story jealously guarded her privileges. But forgiveness cannot be owned, nor can it be jealously guarded as some possession to be used conveniently and only on the terms of one person.

Dorothee Soelle sees in this parable an image of the interdependence of all world systems. "The more that others hang onto the old woman, the more unbreakable the tender little onion becomes. . . . Sharing and communication mean life."[4]

In the political arena, little sharing or genuine communication takes place. Enemies are faceless ideologies. The East fears the "colonial capitalists" while the West is afraid of "totalitarian communism," and terrorism is both an angry act of aggression and attempt by the voiceless to be heard.

Just as there are no formulas for individual forgiving, there are none for addressing global concerns, but the Dostoevsky parable suggests that the destructive hell fire of nuclear war might be averted by a sense of interdependence and mutuality. It was in the woman's best interest that she recognize her relationship to others.

How then might forgiveness be implemented? Perhaps some of the steps for the individual could be applied at an international level.

AN OPPORTUNITY TO BE HONEST

When there is a need for forgiveness, there must be a recognition of a break that requires mending. On an international level, this is most difficult. Nations feel the need to give the appearance of strength. It is a rare occasion for a world leader to confess mistakes of any kind.

The willingness to do so exposes vulnerability which can be interpreted as weakness. But it has happened. At the Democatic National Convention in 1984, Jesse Jackson, a contender for the party's nomination, asked for forgiveness for any pain he might have caused others.

Jackson's statement received a mixed respose. To some delegates it was a "courageous act," to others "a statement of weakness." He did not win his party's nomination, nor his party the election, but for many people Jackson's behavior offered the possibility of a new style of politics.

If, as those who understand forgiveness suggest, accepting one's weaknesses and responsibility for them is a step toward mental health, then a new style of politics is needed in a world of insane acts of terrorism and brutality.

To pretend to be perfect, to always make the right decisions, to never be misled or mistaken, is to set oneself up as God. In the ancient days of "the divine right of kings," wars, murders, and tortures were used to protect leaders. These acts of violence continue, even though the twentieth-century mind rejects "the divine right" of political leaders.

Forgiveness would permit world leaders the opportunity to be honest about their mistakes and to move toward acts of justice as a way of national repentance. It would also free citizens in nations to accept their national broken past.

The year 1985 marked the fortieth anniversary of the end of World War II. Some Christian writers continue to address the issue of corporate guilt regarding the Holocaust and the murder of six million Jews. For many Germans this issue continues to be a shadowy ghost in the political arena. Neo-Nazi groups exist today in a number of countries including Germany, and their presence suggests the need to continue to grapple with the moral issue of the relationship of justice to forgiveness.

In 1940 Dietrich Bonhoeffer, a German theologian later executed by the Nazis, wrote that the only genuine, liberating confession of guilt is that which rejects the temptations of self-justification and rationalization. The separation of individual responsibility from corporate political activity often becomes a means of self-justification.[5]

I can remember my high school American history teacher in Mobile, Alabama. She was a "Daughter of the Confederacy," and the Civil War was still unresolved for her. It was painful to experience her deep antipathy to the North. The humiliation her family had experienced at the end of the war had been passed down from generation to generation. She carried that pain as though it had happened to her. Her pride in her southern heritage was marred by her deep, unforgiving attitude toward the events that followed the war.

Situations similar to that of my teacher had far-reaching social implications in southern cultures. The political and economic issues of the Civil War, the structures of servitude by blacks and poor white people simmered in southern cities.

CHANGING OPPRESSIVE STRUCTURES

Repentance was needed for the acts of slavery. Forgiveness was in order from those who suffered its oppression, for years of misuse of the gospel to support corrupt ideologies, for segregation, and the list goes on. The civil rights issues that came to fruition in the 1960s began another civil war. Small steps to the healing journey of forgiveness began. Dostoevsky's parable was enacted. In southern cities and towns, black and white people began to help pull each other out of the fires of the hell of segregation. Destructive social systems slowly began to be changed.

I remember the discomfort of seeing "white only" signs on drinking fountains at filling stations on dusty highways between Mobile and Brewton, Alabama. I used to wonder as a child where black children got drinks of water, went to the bathroom, or obtained food. In my "white only" culture, individual responsibility was separated from corporate political activity.

Today children in the South watch black families on television programs such as the Bill Cosby show.

These are not the old stereotyped images of black people. There are healthily integrated schools in some parts of southern culture. The systems continue to need changing, but in those arenas where the reality of racial hatred (whether it is white against black or black against white) is denied, the parable of the woman and the onion is reenacted over and over again.

There are still other metaphors that suggest forgiveness is being realized. Several years ago I participated in a wedding in my congregation and stood between a couple and offered a prayer while holding his black hand and her white hand. Many memories flashed through my mind at that moment. I knew that the world, with all its brokenness, was moving toward healing and wholeness.

I did not live in the northern United States until I was an adult. Many of the social problems of the South were just as intense in the cities of the North, yet their existence was denied for years. The South served to shine the light on the bitterness of racial prejudice. The struggles for justice are redemptive when they are seen in the light of the resurrection that follows.

NEW FORMS OF COMMUNITY

Although my own white, middle-class life is a symbol of oppression in many parts of the world, I cannot be a healer by assuming guilt. I can help create justice by acting justly. I can bring about forgiveness by being forgiving.

The world in which I grew up in southern Alabama will be transformed when repentance is acted out in justice. Where people are working to create new forms of liberating community, that world is being transformed, not endured. Transformation creates a new reality.

The recognition of divisions—economic, racial, sexual, political—is the beginning of the journey. For forgiveness to happen, the break must be recognized. I can continue to ignore it, or I can act responsibly to create a new environment. I can pretend the past never happened, or I can own it and move to a new place on my journey.

My nation continues to struggle with all the pain of the Vietnam War. The history of that conflict has been written and rewritten. It has creative possibilities when we recognize its complexity and try to use the pain it brought to stand in a new place.

In a moving article John K. Simmons describes going with his class from the University of California in Santa Barbara to visit the Vietnam Veterans' Memorial in Washington, D.C. He was a teaching assistant in the religious studies department at the university. The group of eighteen included people who, during the war, were conscientious objectors like Simmons, veterans like Wilson and Paul, and others like John Beyer who had not been born when the war began. I believe an understanding of forgiveness as a global principle is evident in Simmons' descriptions of their experience.

Paul elaborated. Vietnam had changed him forever. Feeling the life pass out of a mortally wounded compatriot, seeing starving Vietnamese children fighting over a handful of rice, smelling the stench of death that hung over a napalmed village—all the horrors of war had made the world searingly real for him. For the 17 years since he left Vietnam, it had been practically impossible to adjust to life in the United States. He had stared into the face of death; the American dream was just another nightmare dressed up in a three-piece suit and carrying a gold credit card.

Yet at the wall, Paul had experienced a genuine release from his long-term burden. After the spontaneous ceremony, he had gone off by himself and, sitting under a nearby tree, had cried for hours. There were tears for fallen friends, but, much to Paul's amazement, there were also tears of joy. He had encountered a realness bursting, for once, with hope. In the presence of the wall—a tombstone commemorating the dead—life, paradoxically, seemed not only possible but promising.

He had found his own name on the wall: a John Beyer had given his life in Vietnam at age 20—this student's own age. When he read the name and saw his reflection in the black marble, he was overcome with a sense of his own mortality—as well as the ultimate sacrifice that war demands. His interconnection with this John Beyer, a generation his senior, seemed to extend beyond the sharing of the same name.

But a moment later, despair had yielded to new awareness. The John Beyer on the wall could come alive in the John Beyer who understood the fragility and preciousness of peace and who had touched death and pulled back his hand. Once again, out of death springs new life and purpose.

Wilson's eyes were on fire. "Of course! That's how the wall heals," he said, pounding a fist on the arm rest. "We are all Vietnam veterans—soldiers, conscientious objectors, politicians, protesters—everyone whose life was torn apart by the war. But those whose names are crucified on the wall made the supreme sacrifice. And they are in charge of our resurrection into the real." He continued: "When we stand before the wall, all triviality vanishes. When we complete the circle, the dead on the wall become so much alive, reaching out to the living with this lesson: We all belong to life!"[6]

Forgiveness was part of the healing process at that memorial. To embrace life is to move on the forgiving journey.

Can systems help this process along? Perhaps not. Perhaps most social structures block progress toward peace by mistaking the rhetoric of reconciliation for the activity of reconciliation. But surely if the participants in those organizations are forgivers themselves, the social environment will change.

Judy Small, an Australian folk singer, suggests a way we can look at those with whom we have differences:

And do you think of me as enemy,
And could you call me a friend?
Or will we let our differences
Destroy us in the end?
The wall that stands between us
Could be a window, too.
When I look into the mirror I see you.[7]

It may be that looking at institutions, nations, or groups as separate units restricts the action of forgiving. If, on the other hand, those with whom we disagree or have enmity were the faces we see when we look at our own, might our desires be altered?

To create windows where once there were walls is the work of the Christian disciple. We are enabled to be reconcilers because we have been reconciled to God through Christ: "God, who through Christ reconciled us . . . gave us the ministry of reconciliation; that is, God was in Christ reconciling the world . . . not counting their trespasses against them, and entrusting to us the message of reconciliation" (II Corinthians 5:18–19 RSV).

This Christian power of reconciliation was embodied in Gandhi, the Hindu whose nonviolent call for justice changed the face of the world. In the movie based on his life, there is a moment which incarnates the meaning of forgiveness. Gandhi is near death from a fast to stop the war between Hindu and Muslim tribes. Finally, the tribal leaders agree to a cease-fire and begin bringing their weapons to Gandhi's bedside where they make promises for peace. Into their midst comes a distraught, wild-eyed man who throws bread on Gandhi's bed imploring him to eat. "I'm going to hell and will not take your death with me."

"Only God knows who will go to hell," Gandhi whispers.

Then the man pours out his tale of horror. The Muslims killed his son and he, in turn, killed a Muslim child.

Gandhi listens to the pain-filled story of retribution and says quietly, "I know a way out of hell for you." He urges the man to find a child the size of his own son who was killed. "Raise him as your own son," Gandhi says. "Only be sure to raise him a Muslim."

Gandhi's life was an effort to identify with the broken in his society. Those who might have been his enemies often became his followers. The story illustrates a way of opening "the wall of hostility." How different the story of nations would be if walls became windows between persons with differing religious and political views.

POLITICAL MORALITY

Some theorists strongly object to Christian morality as a possible value in international politics. "Politics cannot be moral," they will say. "Too many cultures have different views of justice." Perhaps this is true. It is also possible that forgiving is not just the domain of Christians but can be found at the center of the truth of all God-centered religions.

There are vast differences in cultures. What works in one may not apply in another. Yet forgiveness might be that quantum leap between cultural differences that will save the planet.

Peter Howard tells of such a quantum leap in his book, *Ideas Have Legs*.

In 1939, two of the most important leaders of the Norwegian Church, Bishop Berggrav and Professor Hallesby, were in conflict, divided by their differing churchmanship and by personal animosity. In the diary of his private prayers the Bishop wrote, "There is a war in Europe. There is also a war between you and Hallesby. Go and see him and make peace for Norway's sake."

Peter Howard believes that this action united the Norwegian churches in their resistance to the Nazis in World War II.

If forgiveness is in the best interest of the forgiver (as the preceding illustrations suggest), then it may be that forgiveness could be adopted as a political position in the "national interest." With the world under the threat of nuclear war, this may be the only political journey that can continue.

Activities

1. Ask two class members to role-play Pope John Paul and Mehmet Ali Agca. Assign them the responsibility a few weeks in advance so that they may research the event. The *Time* magazine article will be available in nearly any public library. Following the role play, ask the class to respond to the following questions:

    a. Was the gesture of the Pope important to world politics?

    b. Where and how can this example be translated into other international events?

    c. How does forgiveness make possible social change?

2. Ask the class members to divide into groups of three and read together the Dostoevsky parable. (One can be the narrator, one the woman, and one the angel.) Discuss forgiveness in light of the parable, as being in the best interest of the forgiver.

3. Distribute newspapers which you have brought to class. Ask participants to find recent news accounts which illustrate the way national leaders use "rationalization and self-justification." (Refer to the Bonhoeffer quote.) Ask them to share these accounts with the class.

4. Now ask class members to meet in groups of six and respond to these questions: Where are there wars still going on between me and another person over some political issues (Vietnam, nuclear disarmament, abortion, the ERA, women in priesthood, etc.)? How can forgiveness work here?

5. Have an old-fashioned debate with one person taking the "pro" side and another the "con" side. "Resolved: Politics can incorporate forgiveness in the decison-making levels of government."
6. Gandhi lived by the following resolutions for each day:

I shall not fear anyone on earth.
I shall fear only God.
I shall not bear ill will toward anyone.
I shall not submit to injustice from anyone.
I shall conquer untruth by truth.
In resisting untruth I shall put up with all suffering.

Have a class member read these resolves and ask participants to discuss them as means of living in forgiveness. What about such resolves makes forgiving possible?
7. Sing together "Lord of All Nations," HS 467.

NOTES

1. Howard Thurman, *The Growing Edge* (New York: Harper & Brothers, 1956), 178–179. Used by permission of Friends United Press. Copyright © 1974 Friends United Press, Richmond, Indiana.
2. Lance Morrow, reported by Barry Kalb and Wilton Wynn/Rome, "I Spoke...As a Brother," *Time* (January 9, 1984): 7–12.
3. Fyodor Dostoevsky, trans. Constance Garnett, *The Brothers Karamazov* (New York: Random House, 1950), 367.
4. Dorothee Soelle, trans. John Sheley, *Political Theology* (Philadelphia: Fortress Press, 1974), 104.
5. Victoria Barnett, "Guilt and Forgiving," *The Christian Century* (September 25, 1985): 833. She refers to Bonhoeffer's writings of 1940.
6. John K. Simmons, "Pilgrimage to the Wall," *The Christian Century* (November 6, 1985): 998. Copyright © 1985 Christian Century Foundation. Reprinted by permission from the Nov. 6, 1985, issue of *The Christian Century*.
7. Judy Small, "Walls and Windows," *One Voice in the Crowd*, Redwood Records, Oakland, California, 1985. Copyright © 1985 Herford Music. All rights reserved. Permission to reprint lyrics granted.

MEDITATION

At the risk of oversimplifying, let me outline the way I have seen my pilgrimage going:

First, I have had to acknowledge, examine, and accept my pains from the past.

Second, I have had to acknowledge, accept, and appreciate the gifts that I have received through the grace of God and the grace of other persons.

Third, I have had to make crucial decisions.

Fourth, I have had to become able to trust the persons who are important to me, whom I call "my significant others."

—Maxie Dunnam[1]

*　　　*　　　*

Forgive yourself for past mistakes

Let them go from your mind...the only place they ever were...hanging on like gnawing aches that spoil your present experience of life.

Stop imposing the agony of remorse on yourself, and see yourself acting back then as a child...without insight...without maturity.

You have grown since. The mistakes contributed to that growth. You would not act the same way now.

You cannot change the past...but you can change your thoughts about it.

An attitude is ours to control.

We are the creators.

Change your thoughts and you change your world.

—Kristin Zambrucka[2]

Chapter 7

The Forgiver—Cartographer of Healing

Goals of this session:*
- To establish the individual responsibility to plot the forgiving journey
- To acknowledge some helpful directions
- To explore scriptural models

Objectives:
- Participants will create a map of forgiveness from a personal experience in the past.
- An exercise in "letting go" will be practiced.
- A "burnt offering" activity will demonstrate the sacramental use of forgiven hurts.
- Participants will write a Psalm of Forgiveness.
- The Bread of Forgiveness will be shared.

---

*Note to teacher: Class activities will require advance preparation. Assignments will need to be given to participants the week before each class session.

When I leave on a trip, I often pick up a "trip ticket" from my local automobile association. This is a segment of a larger map which has my route charted according to distance and time. It helps me plan my itinerary. I know how many miles there are between stops I might want to make. I have information about certain historical places near the various points. I can determine how much time I want to allow between stops on my journey.

There are no "trip tickets" for forgiveness. The journey is unique to each forgiver, and while the work of many people who are forgivers can be helpful, the map for the journey must be created by the one who makes it.

MAKING OUR MAPS

This is why one might call a forgiver a cartographer, a map maker. The cartographer studies all that can be learned about the terrain and sets out to create a map that will help other travelers. So it is with one who makes the forgiving journey. What is learned can benefit others.

We begin the pilgrimage of forgiveness recognizing that we have been placed in relationships. Life on this earth is brief. Those persons who touch our lives can enrich us or cause us pain. But if we sense our interdependency the possibility of forgiving is increased. So, we start out recognizing the fragility of all life. We can offer this ancient Aztec prayer:

Oh, only for so short a time you have loaned us to each other
Because you take form in your act of drawing us, and we take life in your painting us, and we breathe in your singing us.

But only for a short time you have loaned us to each other.

Because even a drawing cut in crystalline obsidian fades. And even the green feathers, the crown feathers, of the quetzal bird lose their color, and even the sounds of the waterfall die out in the dry season.

So, we too, because only for a short while have you loaned us to each other.[3]

Forgiveness helps us value others. For we have been given to each other to draw light from one another, to shine in dark places of nonforgiveness by our willingness to address that which separates us and to stand together against the darkness.

I believe that there are refreshment places on a journey which help a traveler move forward, like a good night's rest after a long day's trip. There are also difficult spots on a journey that require skill to avoid risk and danger. But each of the points on a journey is a good place if one is willing to travel.

Perhaps, then, a pilgrimage of forgiving begins by asking the question, "What do I want?" Some may need to ask, "Do I want to continue to carry this weight of anger, antipathy, rejection, distance, separation, hurt, humiliation, pain? Do I really want the weight lifted? Do I want to pay the price of moving beyond where I am now? Am I willing to risk finding a new identity beyond this one of being the offender or offended?" And finally, the pilgrim may need to ask, "Where do I start?"

One certainty is that early in the journey the traveler must let go of a lot of "garbage" from the past. Often that garbage started out as justifiable anger or hurt. Now, held on to and used as a shield to avoid relationships, it is of little value.

This ancient rabbinic story illustrates the value of letting go.

Once upon a time there was a man who lived on an island. He loved the island; it was his home, his land. It had given him and his family all that they had needed throughout his life. One day as he lay dying, he stretched out in the sun on the earth of his island. He grasped a handful of his beloved land and died. The story says that when he arrived at heaven's gate, he was clasping, in each hand, soil of his land.

"Sorry," the gatekeeper told him. You can bring nothing into heaven. You'll have to leave that handful of earth outside."

The man refused to enter. Time passed and he sat outside of the gates of heaven grasping the earth of his beloved island. He would not part with this that had meant so much to him.

The story says that one day God came out to the bench where the old man sat and tried to persuade him to throw away the dirt and come into heaven. The man was not persuaded, and God walked sorrowfully away.

Then a young child came out to the bench, the story says, walked around the old man who was, by now, clasping dry dust in his hands. The days of clinging to the soil had reduced it to dust—all its rich life was gone.

The child climbed on to the old man's lap and said, "Old man, don't you know that you can only come into heaven with empty hands."

The story says that the old man realized suddenly that he was holding on to dust. He flung out his hand, clasped the hand of the child and walked through the gates of heaven where it is said he found all the treasures of his heart—all that he had valued on the earth.[4]

This may be the first mark on the legend as we make our map. The key is letting go. The rabbinic story is a parable of what we do when we start our forgiving journey. The scholar William Gesenius, in his *Hebrew and Chaldee Lexicon,* states that the Old

Testament word for forgiveness is *shalach,* which has a primary meaning to lighten or to lift up.

Letting go lightens the load we carry on the journey. It gives us greater freedom to move. Another writer has suggested that the words in the Old Testament for forgiveness are power words. "Sin is covered, put behind God's back so that it no longer stands in the way of a free exchange of love. Or it is carried away so that the road is open."[5] Recently, when I shared these ideas with a friend, she began to laugh. "It is funny," she said, "that you would put the two ideas in that sequence. I was not able to value the person who hurt me until I let go of the past. One night I stood at the kitchen sink preparing apples for canning. As I peeled them and cut out the imperfections, I realized that some resentments I held toward another woman were eating at me like the bad spots had harmed the apples. I remember gathering up all the garbage from the apples and taking it out to the compost heap. I stood there, with tears running down my cheeks, and let go of the past. Until I had done that I could not reach out to this woman and begin the journey of forgiveness with her."

My friend was a cartographer of forgiving. The first markings on her map were made by letting go.

If this exercise is too difficult, we might practice Judy Small's advice (page 113) and try to see the face of the one who has offended us when we look at our own reflection in the mirror.

To be truly human, we must be in relationship. The people who wound us contribute to our development just as surely as those who love us. "Because we are sinners both against God and others, we cannot realize ourselves unless others forgive our sins by restoring our relationship to them. Others cannot be re-created unless we forgive them,"[6] writes Bernard Loomer. The imperative is forgiveness both *from* others and *to* others.

This means taking the sin of another into myself. But that is what the offense may have been. The life of Jesus and those who have acted in Christian discipleship are rich in examples of this capacity to "bear the burdens of another's sin."

A Pharisee invited Jesus to have dinner with him. Jesus went to his house and sat down to eat. There was a woman in that town who lived a sinful life. She heard that Jesus was eating in the Pharisee's house so she brought an alabaster jar full of perfume and stood behind Jesus, by his feet, crying and wetting his feet with her tears. Then she dried his feet with her hair, kissed them and poured the perfume on them. When the Pharisee who had invited Jesus saw this, he said to himself, "If this man were really a prophet, he would know who this woman is who is touching him; he would know what kind of sinful life she leads!" Jesus spoke up and said to him, "Simon, I have something to tell you.... There were two men who owed money to a money lender.... One owed him five hundred dollars and the other one fifty dollars. Neither one could pay him back, so he canceled the debts of both. Which one, then will love him more?" "I suppose," answered Simon, "that it would be the one who was forgiven more." "Your answer is correct" said Jesus. Then he turned to the woman and said to Simon, "Do you see this woman? I came into your home and you gave me no water for my feet, but she has washed my feet with her tears and dried them with her hair. You did not welcome me with a kiss, but she has not stopped kissing my feet since I came. You provided no oil for my head, but she has covered my feet with perfume. I tell you...the great love she has shown proves that her many sins have been forgiven. Whoever has been forgiven little, however, shows only a little love." Then Jesus said to the woman, "Your sins are forgiven."[7]

When I read this story, I am struck by the intense love that the woman showed Jesus. His forgiving spirit enabled the overflow of her heart to be expressed. He saw her as a healer as well as one who was healed; the Pharisee saw her as an object, an illness.

This story emphasizes the correlation between the capacity to love and the willingness to give and receive forgiveness. Jesus' love exceeded the limitations of the law; he could forgive. The woman's love extended beyond the circumscribed role of her society; she could accept forgiveness. The burdens of Jesus' fatigue and physical needs were lifted by the woman; the burden of sin of the woman was lifted by Jesus.

Another symbol on our map's legend, then, is that of accepting our own sin as forgiven, so that we may continue traveling. Our capacity to love is grounded in our acceptance of forgiveness. The depth of our love is founded on both the giving and receiving of forgiveness which is God's action. "Only God can forgive," wrote Paul Tillich who believed that only in God are love and justice completely united.[8]

GOD FORGIVES

The paradox is that we are often unable to accept God's forgiveness to us until we have been willing to extend forgiveness to another. When we pray the Lord's prayer, we say, "Forgive us our trespasses, as we forgive those who trespass against us."[9] Just as the parable of the unforgiving servant illustrates, to be unforgiving to others blocks God's forgiveness to us. We set in motion, by our acts of forgiving, the divine promise of forgiveness in our own lives.

The writer of Hebrews reminds the early Christians of the promise of God to Jeremiah: "This is the covenant that I will make...says the Lord: I will put my laws into their minds, and write them on their hearts....I will be merciful toward their iniquities and I will remember their sins no more." The Hebrew writer continues. "Where there is forgiveness of these, there is no longer any offering for sin."[10]

The forgiveness of God has been expressed to us in the life, death, and resurrection of Jesus Christ. When we refuse to forgive, we deny ourselves the promise of that resurrecting power in our own lives. Another New Testament writer reminds us that to live in this promise is to experience light in the midst of darkness. We might look at unforgiveness as blinding us to the light of God's forgiveness and remember this:

If we say we have fellowship with [God] while we walk in darkness, we lie and do not live according to the truth; but if we walk in the light, as Christ is in the light, we have fellowship with one another, and the blood of Jesus... cleanses us from all sin. If we say we have no sin, we deceive ourselves, and the truth is not in us. If we confess our sins, God is faithful and just, and will forgive our sins and cleanse us from all unrighteousness.[11]

So another helpful key to the journey of forgiveness is to accept God's forgiveness for my own sin and move toward acted-out forgiveness to another. This builds a lifestyle of mutuality. If I recognize that I am a sinner when I am hurt by another's sin, then I realize we are equal in God's sight, and God's love has forgiven us both. I am then freed to forgive the other person.

This mutuality is another part of the legend of my map. "I found out that I could forgive my father who deserted our family," the man said. "I had to face the awful truth that he did not love me; that he left because he chose to. I had to accept the fact that he made no further contact with our family because he had no desire to know us.

"That is a horrible, painful truth to face, but one I could finally accept. I could say out loud, 'My father did not love me.' Perhaps he wanted to and couldn't, but he did not. I no longer felt that I had to excuse him or lie about him. The stories I created that somehow he wanted to be with us but someone kept him away could be set aside. I did not need them any more.

"I am now free to love and live in the present. I am now able to love the child in me that my father could not love. By loving that child in myself, I am now able to love the man that I am today, and in a strange way love the man who was no father to me, but was a broken human being loved of God."

MUTUAL EMPOWERMENT

This willingness to accept rejection and realize that the longed-for physical reconciliation would never happen, permitted this man to develop a unique style of mutuality. He was able to give the child in himself the love that his father could not, and once that began to happen he was able to love more creatively as an adult.

Often the child in many adults keeps punishing the adult because there is such a hunger for love and acceptance. But the forgiver remembers the Apostle Paul's testimony, "Where sin abounded, grace did much more abound."[12] Where a human being can learn to accept responsibility for whatever life has given and love the broken child inside, the power of forgiveness offers a new form of mutual empowerment. Both the past and the present are united in a new place. The past person—forgiven and freed from alienation—is united with the person in the present who is liberated to move forward.

FREEDOM FOR THE FUTURE

Many more keys might be placed on the map. As you move on your journey, discover how you can use your own understanding to become a forgiver. Sometimes others will not understand, but remember that forgiving is often the soundest action you can make for your own mental health. One woman discovered this and was able to forgive in a way that few people can.

A man and woman had a daughter who was brutally assaulted and murdered. The parents were required to go through the horror of the trial, to be exposed to the crime over and over again through the media.

Finally, the murderer was found guilty and sentenced to life imprisonment with no opportunity for parole. The couple tried to begin their life again.

Day after day the mother of the murdered young woman would recall the event. She was unable to continue her employment. She sought the help of a physician, a therapist. Her husband was grieving, too, but the woman was on the verge of emotional and physical collapse. One day, as she moved through the house, she thought, I must go see that man and forgive him.

She was uncertain as to her husband's response, but when she began to explain how desperate she was to let go of the past, he agreed.

They wrote a letter to the prison official and to the murderer requesting an opportunity to meet with him. The request was granted. She described the fear that she felt as they made their trip to the prison.

When they were permitted to see the man, he could not look in their eyes, but with tears streaming, she choked out her offer of forgiveness. "I must let this go," she said. "The only way I can do it is to offer you our forgiveness." The man looked up in wonderment, nodded his head, and left the room.

Later, when she shared this with others, she was criticized. "How could you do this?" friends asked. "You have trivialized your daughter's life," another critic said.

The woman was convinced, however. "I did not do it for that man. I loved my daughter beyond human comprehension. But you have to understand—I was losing my mind. I was not freed of the horror of that event until I had forgiven the murderer. I didn't forgive for him. I forgave to save my sanity. I had to, don't you see?"

Forgiveness may be the only way to "save" ourselves from the bondage of despair, of physical distress, of hatred and accompanying sorrow. That woman knew her limits and trusted herself enough to risk such pain.

Whatever wounds I carry, I must decide how to free myself from their damaging hold on me. I can look at the legacy that forgivers have left. I can study the routes they have taken. I can look carefully at the journeys. I can look, too, at the nonforgivers, stuck in their bogs of despair and frustration. They also offer me maps. My friend in the supermarket often comes to my mind. I would never want to carry the baggage she struggles with every day. Whatever the pain and risk, forgivers seem to have more freedom. The forgivers in my own history, the forgivers in literature, and those stalwarts of the faith for whom forgiveness became a way of being offer me hope.

Forgivers show me by the spirit of peace which graces their lives that the journey is worthwhile. Their maps, sometimes tattered from much use, are like treasure maps of ancient lore. They have led the traveler to riches beyond imaginings, and I want to go on that treasure hunt with them.

It is time to begin map making!

Activities

1. Members of the class can list six steps to take on their forgiving journey.
2. Using the idea of the map from session 5 and the Augsburger chart from session 1, determine which of the many models suggested is most useful to you. Begin a new map incorporating your six steps.
3 Each member of the class will receive a 3" x 5" card. Ask each person to write on the card some hurt that needs forgiving. Then collect the cards and place them in a receptacle in which they can be burned. (A small, portable barbecue grill or a cast iron skillet on a trivet will work.) Place all the cards together and set them afire. As they burn remind the class members that the Holy Spirit is symbolized by flame and by smoke. Perhaps this exercise can remind the class of the power of the Holy Spirit to move into a hurt and transform it.
4. Allow about ten minutes for a psalm-writing exercise. Ask the class members to compose a short psalm.

Here are a couple of examples:

God who suffers with us,
The weight of despair pierced
   us like thorns against our tender flesh.
The aching agony of lonely struggle
   bound us to a cross of loneliness.
But in the crisis of our crucifixion
   You were present.
Now we are an Easter people.
   The morning of our resurrection dawns slowly
   and we waken to the lifting of the pain.

God of our every moment
God of our torn-flesh past
We are risen with you.
And the cross stands empty.
Now we are an Easter people.[13]

We are forgiven, reconciled, healed.
Lord, those are such big words,
hard to understand.
I want to believe that I am forgiven....
Forgive me, Lord.
Give me strength and courage
    to start again,
to choose your way instead of mine....
Lord, you and I are partners
    working together for your glory.
It is not me against you.
It is us together.[14]

5. Take time to share the psalms.
6. Seated in a circle, as a final exercise, read aloud together HS 424, "Send Me Forth, O Blessed Master."

    Then break a loaf of bread and tear off a small portion. Give it to the person to your right, saying, "May the bread of God's forgiveness feed you, nourish you, and come alive in your life." Ask each member of the class to share the bread in the same way and repeat the benedictory blessing.
7. Close with a prayer and the singing of "Freely, Freely," HS 382, and "Creator of Sunrises," HS 186.

NOTES

1. Maxie Dunnam, *alive now!* (September/October 1975): 63. Copyright © 1975 *The Upper Room*. Used by permission.
2. Kristin Zambrucka, *Ano Ano: The Seed* (Makiki, Hawaii: Mana Publishing, 1971). Used by permission.
3. Edward Hays, *Secular Sanctity* (New York: Paulist Press, 1980), 106.
4. From a lecture by Belden C. Lane at Eden Seminary, St. Louis, Missouri. Also may be found on *Storytelling: The Enchantment of Theology*, a series of tapes by Belden C. Lane, produced by Bethany Press (St. Louis, Missouri, 1981). Used by permission of Bethany Press.
5. Alan Webster, *Broken Bones May Joy: Studies in Reconciliation and Resurrection* (London: SCM Press Ltd., 1968), 10.
6. Bernard Loomer, "Christian Faith and Process Philosophy," *Process Philosophy and Christian Thought*, Delwin Brown, Ralph E. James, and Gene Reeves, eds. (Indianapolis: Bobbs, Merrill Company, 1971), 70–98.
7. Luke 7:36–48 TEV.
8. Paul Tillich, *Love, Power and Justice* (London: Oxford University Press, 1954), 121.
9. Matthew 6:13 IV.
10. Hebrews 8:10–12 and 10:18 RSV.
11. I John 1:5–9 (adapted).
12. Romans 5:20 IV.
13. Barbara Howard, "Psalm for Today," *Restoration Witness* (July/August 1985).
14. Jean Croker Petke in *alive now!* (May/June, 1982):50. Copyright © 1982 *The Upper Room*. Used by permission.

PHOTO CREDITS

Bibliography

Books

Arendt, Hannah. *The Human Condition.* Chicago: University of Chicago Press, 1970.

Auden, W. H. *Another Time.* New York: Random House, 1948.

Augsburger, David. *Caring Enough to Forgive/Caring Enough to Not Forgive.* Ventura, California: Regal Books, 1981.

Bonhoeffer, Dietrich. *Life Together.* Translated by John W. Doberstein. New York: Harper and Row, 1954.

———. *Ethics.* Edited by Eberhard Bethge. New York: Macmillan and Company, 1965.

Boulding, Maria. *The Coming of God.* Collegeville, Minnesota: Liturgical Press, 1983.

Brown, Delwin, Ralph E. James, and Gene Reeves, eds. *Process Philosophy and Christian Thought.* Indianapolis: Bobbs and Merrill, 1971.

Buechner, Frederick. *A Room Called Remember— Uncollected Pieces.* San Francisco: Harper and Row, 1984.

Cargas, Harry James. *In Conversation with Elie Wiesel.* New York: Paulist Press, 1976.

Donnelly, Doris. *Learning to Forgive.* New York: Macmillan Publishing Company, 1979.

———. *Putting Forgiveness into Practice.* Allen, Texas: Argus Communication, 1982.

Dostoevsky, Fyodor. *The Brothers Karamazov.* Translated by Constance Garnett. New York: Random House, 1950.

Emswiler, Sharon, and Thomas Neufer Emswiler. *Women and Worship.* San Francisco: Harper & Row Publishing, 1980.

Guest, Judith. *Ordinary People*. New York: Ballantine Books, 1976.

Hong, Edna. *Forgiveness Is a Work as Well as a Grace*. Minneapolis: Augsburg Publishing House, 1984.

Hoyer, Robert. *Seventy Times Seven*. Nashville, Abingdon, 1976.

Jampolsky, Gerald. *Goodbye to Guilt*. New York: Bantam, 1985.

Klassen, William. *The Forgiving Community*. Philadelphia: Westminster Press, 1966.

Lambert, Jean. *The Human Action of Forgiving: A Critical Application of the Metaphysics of Alfred North Whitehead*. Lanham, Maryland: University Press of America, 1985.

L'Engle, Madeleine. *The Summer of the Great-Grandmother*. New York: Farrar, Straus and Giroux, 1974.

Lewis, Clive Staples. *The Last Battle*. New York: Macmillan Publishing Company, 1962.

Lifton, Robert Jay. *Death in Life: Survivors of Hiroshima*. New York: Simon and Schuster, 1976.

——. *The Broken Connection*. New York: Simon and Schuster, 1979.

Linn, Dennis, and Mathew Linn. *Healing Life's Hurts*. New York: Paulist Press, 1978.

Peck, Scott. *The Road Less Traveled*. New York: Harcourt, Brace and Company, 1978.

Piercy, Marge. *Circles on the Water: Selected Poems of Marge Piercy*. New York: Alfred Knopf, 1982.

Smede, Lewis. *Forgive and Forget*. San Francisco: Harper and Row, 1984.

Soelle, Dorothee, trans. John Sheley. *Political Theology*. Philadelphia: Fortress Press, 1974.

Spencer, Geoffrey. *Strangers and Pilgrims.* Independence, Missouri: Herald House, 1984.

ten Boom, Corrie with John and Elizabeth Sherrill. *The Hiding Place.* Chappaqua, New York: Chosen Books Inc., 1971.

Thompson, Murray Stewart. *Grace and Forgiveness in Ministry.* Nashville: Abingdon, 1981.

Tillich, Paul. *Love, Power and Justice.* London: Oxford University Press, 1954.

———. *The Shaking of the Foundations.* New York: Charles Scribner's Sons, 1948.

———. *Theology of Culture.* London: Oxford University Press, 1959.

Thurman, Howard. *The Growing Edge.* Richmond, Indiana: Friends United Press, 1974.

Tournier, Paul. *The Strong and the Weak.* Translated by Edwin Hudson. Philadelphia: Westminster Press, 1963.

Webster, Alan. *Broken Bones May Joy; Studies in Reconciliation and Resurrection.* London: SCM Press Ltd., 1968.

Westerhoff, John H. *The Spiritual Life: Learning East and West.* Minneapolis, Minnesota: Winston Press, Seabury, 1982.

Zambrucka, Kristin. *Ano Ano: The Seed.* Makiki, Hawaii: Mana Publishing, 1971.

Other References

Barnett, Victoria. "Guilt and Forgiving." *The Christian Century* (September 25, 1985): 833.

Garrison, Louise. "Where Was God?—A Journey of Healing." *Sojourners* 13, no. 10 (November 1984): 23.

Howard, Barbara. "Psalm for Today." *Restoration Witness*, (July/August 1985).

Lane, Belden C. *Storytelling: the Enchantment of Theology.* St. Louis, Missouri: Bethany Press, 1981.

Loomer, Bernard. "Two Kinds of Power." *Criterion* (Winter 1976): 27.

Morrow, Lance, Reported by Barry Kalb and Wilton Wynn/Rom. "I Spoke...As a Brother." *Time* (January 9, 1984): 7–12.

Petke, Jean Croker. *alive now!* (May/June 1982): 50.

Reagon, Bernice Johnson. "Sweet Honey in the Rock," Soundtrack Wilmington 10 U.S.A., Songtalk Publishing Company, 1979.

Simmons, John K. "Pilgrimage to the Wall." *The Christian Century* (November 6, 1985): 998.

Small, Judy. "Walls and Windows." *One Voice in the Crowd*, Redwoods Records, Oakland, California, 1985.

Spong, John Shelby. "Can the Church Bless Divorce?" *Christian Century* (November 28, 1984): 1126.

Wiebe, Elizabeth. "Rahab, I'd Like to Talk to You." *The Mennonite* (July 3, 1946): 336.

Willimon, William. "Endings and Beginnings." *alive now!* (September/October 1979): 38–39.